THE MIDLIFE MALE

amplifypublishing.com

The Midlife Male: A No-Bullshit Guide to Living Better,
Longer, Happier, Healthier, and Wealthier and Having More
Fun in Your 40s and 50s (Which Includes More Sex ...
and What Guy Doesn't Want That?)

For more information, please contact:
Amplify Publishing
620 Herndon Parkway #320
Herndon, VA 20170
info@amplifypublishing.com

CPSIA Code: PRV0522A
Library of Congress Control Number: 2022901327
ISBN-13: 978-1-63755-417-3

Printed in the United States

To:

My father—*the ultimate Midlife Male*

My boys—*my "why" for everything I do*

And especially Kate—*who continually pushes me to be the partner she deserves, has changed my game for the better since the day I met her, and gave me the opportunity to become a father*

THE MIDLIFE MALE

A No-Bullshit Guide to Living Better,
Longer, Happier, Healthier, and
Wealthier and Having More Fun
in Your 40s and 50s

*(Which Includes More Sex ...
and What Guy Doesn't Want That?)*

GREG SCHEINMAN

CONTENTS

What is the "Midlife Male"?

(August 3, 2017, MidlifeMale.com)

I've been working on this idea for a while now. It's called "Midlife Male". What is the midlife Male. He's a guy @35-55 balancing work, life, family, health/fitness, finance/money, some style/fashion - trying to balance it all and live his best life possible without regret. He's about having both substance and style. About punching the bully in the mouth. About experiences over things. He's about quality over quantity. He's about learning and living. About trying, failing and ultimately succeeding. He's about questioning things. He's not trying to fit in or conform. He's into iconic, classic, timeless style. He's about being a great father. About understanding that there are no things more valuable than time, health and family. He's about knowing when enough is enough. He is about perseverance, discipline and having fun.

I'm going to talk to other midlife males on my podcast. Blog about fitness, food, fashion, family, finance - not to provide advice or come at this like in any kind of expert but rather that we're all in this together, just trying to do our best, be our best and be happy, secure and comfortable in our own skin - Midlife Male is a lifestyle for like minded guys just trying to figure it all out.

Just hoping to inspire, aspire and perspire together...

PREFACE

Those 222 words are the first blog post I ever wrote at MidlifeMale.com, complete with the requisite photo of my family—my two boys, Auden and Harper, who now look considerably older as they are fast approaching manhood, and my amazing wife of twenty years, Kate, who hasn't aged a day. This was posted August 3, 2017.

I reprinted it here because the content remains rock solid with where I'm standing four years later as I write this book.

The post is not perfect. I see a few questionable punctuation choices and at least two glaring typos. Maybe it's too short. Maybe it's incomplete. Maybe I didn't develop a narrative arc. I don't give a damn. Its purpose remains as true as ever, and so does the intent behind it. Why wouldn't I put in the flaws? That's the best representation of what this book and the Midlife Male are about.

If there's one thing you should know about me, it's that I'm all about putting the imperfections out there for the world to see. I put myself on display every week, through words, through hosting a podcast, through social media posts and photos. Even when I think I'm looking good, I see those imperfections. I'm like you: I sometimes question my motivations, confidence, and abilities. I may think I'm fooling others, but I'm not fooling myself. What I do is take action anyway, to the best of my abilities. No regrets. Join me now in maximizing midlife.

Midlife: Crisis or sweet spot?

The phrase "midlife crisis" was coined by Elliott Jaques in 1965 in an attempt to capture the shift in identity and self-confidence that occurs as we transition to the next stage of life. It's associated with anxiety, depression, resentment, remorse, a desire for drastic and desperate change, and generally other things that suck.

But it doesn't have to be.

For too long, midlife has been considered the end. I'm saying it's prime time. Some guys handle a midlife crisis—man, I hate that term—by getting a yellow Porsche. I'm writing a book. Why? It's not because I think I have all the answers. It's because I want to be part of a team of like-minded men who are committed to living our best lives for ourselves and our loved ones.

I started my Midlife Male podcast for a simple, ostensibly selfish reason. Inviting inspirational, high-performing, interesting guests to the show gave me an excuse to have a conversation and learn from others about how I could be a better man as I approach my fifties.

In the process, I realized how much I liked listening and learning. The podcast ignited my curiosity and empowered me to apply what I could from their successes and mistakes. Why wouldn't I choose to explore the experience of figuring out work, life, family, health, fitness, money, and style with people who graciously share what they've discovered on their way to becoming experts in these areas?

Each podcast interview is like my own personal MBA, a conversation with a mentor or coach I could have used decades ago but still can learn from now. There's no reason you shouldn't get the same opportunity. Why should I be the only one fortunate enough to talk with these guys for an hour? If you get just one takeaway from each podcast (now over 150 episodes and counting!)—a life hack, a meaningful story, an excuse to share the interview with someone you haven't connected with in a while, a new perspective on the world—what difference could that make in your life?

My newsletter and Instagram posts allow me to share the roller coaster of my week, to vent and commiserate with subscribers and followers for a few hundred words.

On all of these platforms and in my personal experience, I can tell you with complete confidence that the middle is not the end. It's the sweet spot, the beginning of the next and best phase of our lives. We're playing the long game, living longer and more positively, learning more and applying it every single day.

This book

I'm humbled by my guests, and I also know that I've got lots of successes and mistakes that I can contribute to help guide other men. That's where this book comes in. It combines the listening and throwing up into a handy companion sized for your back pocket.

This book will help you boost your confidence, curiosity, and creativity as you make the most of middle age. I want men to live their best lives, authentically and unapologetically. The good news is we aren't in this alone. I talk with men every week to help me find ways and better understanding of how—repeat, *how*—to do just that.

I'm serious about connecting with other men and helping them bring out their best. My professional journey has been unconventional, to say the least. I ended my first job out of college by telling Harvey Weinstein to fuck off. I sold my entertainment business to Michael Eisner in my thirties. But other aspects of my professional and personal lives are fairly standard and similar to what many men go through by the time they reach their forties and fifties. I've been broke and wealthy, happy and manically depressed, competitive-level fit and completely off kilter with my priorities. I lost my father in my teens, my brother was in prison, and I've struggled with alcohol, body image, anxiety, and self-confidence.

I'm now forty-nine. I've regained my health and have made a pivot in business and in life. The Midlife Male Movement helps me and many others find that elusive balance we all strive for. I'm going to be perfectly clear that balance is a fallacy. People talk about balance as the ultimate goal, but can we just be honest that certain aspects of your life must take priority at certain times, and that means other areas will suffer? That's the truth. How to juggle that conundrum makes all the difference.

Considering the many different roles we all play, we have a never-ending stream of decisions and needs tugging at us. That can create strained relationships, challenges to navigate, and misplaced goals. I've been a filmmaker, a sports video producer, a TV host, a fitness studio owner, an insurance broker, a performance coach, a CrossFit coach, a triathlete, a decathlete, a friend, a father, a husband, a brother, and a son. We all lose our way sometimes. But pursuing your passions and happiness while maintaining your integrity and responsibilities are why it's worth getting back on track.

Whatever your age or your financial or relationship situation, it's not too late to find success on your terms. I know you've made some mistakes, and I also know you've done some things right. The big question is how you're going to make the years you have left count.

This book is my story, in part, but I hope it's also a model for others in my Midlife Male demographic or those who will be there someday. This is my invitation to you to clean your house. Come out, slim down, bulk up, reach higher, dig deeper... whatever you need, the people you'll meet in these pages have been there. We're a community working together to help each other.

Portfolio of your life allocations

You'll notice that I don't have the same number of chapters in each of the six Fs that make up this book and our lives: Family, Fitness, Finance, Food, Fashion, and Fun.

We all have to emphasize different areas at different periods in our lives. Your mileage may vary. Don't let yourself get obsessed with finding perfect balance—it ain't happening. And it doesn't need to happen. Consider the six Fs a pie chart that shows your portfolio of life allocations. Like your investment portfolio, you need to make regular adjustments to get the best results. That pie is going to be lopsided at times. Just remember these three things:

1) Many of these chapters are relevant across other Fs too. Not only is that pie going to be lopsided, it's going to be loaded with Venn diagrams. Life's like that. It can get messy.

2) If you do want more on a particular F, check out my podcasts, follow me on Instagram, and subscribe to my weekly newsletter at MidlifeMale.com. My guests and I are always talking about one or more of these in any given piece.

3) Do yourself a favor and don't keep getting so much better at the Fs that are your strengths that you don't address the Fs that could benefit from your attention. Maybe having that conversation with your son is more important than another fifteen pounds on your bench press. Maybe booking a family vacation next month is more important than polishing to perfection that monthly report that no one will ever read. You hear me? Good for you if the grades on your report card for some of your Fs are outstanding. Just be willing to turn some of the other Fs into As too.

Most of all, I want you to step into your own life and find success the way *you* define it. It's later now than it was when you first became a man, but so what? It's not too late. And, significantly, you have a lot more experience to draw on, and you're taking on responsibilities that back then you just gave the middle finger to. You're better than that now. I know I am ... and I'm not at the end of my journey.

"We're all in this together," I wrote in that first post, "just trying to do our best, be our best and be happy, secure and comfortable in our own skin—Midlife Male is a life-style for like-minded guys just trying to figure it all out."

My blog posts have more proofreading now, and my podcasts have higher production quality, but that statement remains as true today as it was then.

INTRODUCTION

The Man in the Mirror

What do you see when you get out of the shower and stand in front of a mirror? The good, the bad, or the ugly?

I hope you celebrate the good, forgive the bad, and acknowledge the ugly. Because it's all you, and accepting *that* is my prescription for building your future. Day one, step one starts now.

Take off the towel and let it all hang out. Yeah, you might find some things you don't like. Check out those gray hairs that weren't there last year, the sun spots and sagging tattoos from decades ago. How about that scar that's never going away and more wrinkles creeping in? Why do I have no hair there and so much hair sprouting over here? And damn, is my junk really hanging that low?

Don't stop there though. Embrace what looks good. Find that definition when you flex your arms and legs. Stand up a little taller, and see a sparkle in your eyes when you bring a smile to the surface—even if your teeth are a little more yellow than you want. And actually, that scar is kinda badass, even if the story of how you got it isn't.

What about what you don't see? Your brain, your heart, your soul—all that's beneath this exterior that you don't see in the mirror but you sure as hell know is reflected back at you. Would your younger self be proud of what you see and what you feel now?

Can you fit into clothes from five years ago? How about twenty-five years ago? Do you not care? Do you care too much?

Some people say it's a trap: if you look in the mirror, you'll see all your flaws. I say put yourself on display. It's just you, man. It's just you. Be honest with yourself now so you can be authentic when your clothes are on. These questions are not about finding extremes—neither your perceived flaws that you have to fix, nor plotting your next Instagram post or dating app profile. It's about being real with yourself, knowing what you've got as well as what ain't coming back. It's really about knowing what you want to project, what you want to achieve, and assessing how to get there.

Who do you want to see looking back at you?

You may think you know what's coming next in a book like this—some rah-rah drill-sergeant shit to push you to lose the tire around your waist, get ripped, and lengthen and strengthen your rod.

Let me stop you right there. If you want to look and feel different, then I'm with you, brother. Whether you're jacked or you've lost the edge you once had, whether you've seized the day or sabotaged yourself, we've all got work we can do, and we all have parts of our lives to be proud of. This book is about deciding which is which and how to go about living our best lives in our best bodies that house our best selves.

The next time you get out of the shower, find a mirror—full length, if you can. Am I asking you to be naked and afraid? Not at all. I'm inviting you to be naked and aware.

Check yourself out

The truth is, mirrors and reflections are inescapable. In your bathroom, at the gym, at work, or at restaurants, maybe the reflection in the window or water is showing you in a certain light. We see mirrors, broken and intact, in movies, music videos, and all kinds of places—the *Twilight Zone* opening, Billy Joel's *Glass Houses*, Michael Jackson's "Man in the Mirror." They're revealing but can be deceptive and mysterious.

Lots of people try to avoid mirrors or put filters on the photos so they can only be seen a certain way. The rest of the images get deleted. Stop letting those chances for honesty slip by, and take a hard, raw look at yourself. They are opportunities to take stock of how you show up to the world. Better to grab hold of them rather than try to ignore them. As Jackson Browne sang, "No matter how fast I run, I can never seem to get away from me."

There are no right or wrong reasons for checking yourself out. Everyone else is, just as you're checking others out. We're human beings, after all ... constantly assessing and judging our surroundings for the sake of curiosity, safety, connection, revenge. The real question for you is what you want and expect for yourself, and that means doing more than just admiring your pecs and abs; look inward at where your heart and head are.

I'll tell you straight up that I love a lot of what I see now when I look in the mirror and inside myself. It's a daily journey to make sure I continue to do so. I've spent a lot of time in gyms through the years, and I know some of that commitment wasn't healthy. I didn't know it at the time, but I was dealing with body dysmorphia. I could never do enough reps or find a perfect enough workout to cover up the blemishes I saw when I looked in that locker room mirror. I take photos without a shirt now, and what I see is a lot of hard work that I'm proud to show off. But with that kind of history, I know all my mistakes, anxieties, and quirks that I battle in order to love myself. Looking in the mirror motivates me to make changes; it also offers me an opportunity to show myself grace.

You're going to see me return to this image of the mirror throughout the book, and I'll reveal what I see in myself. There's no time to waste in holding up the mirror to yourself too.

Reclaim your masculinity

A Midlife Male strives for purpose and joy, accepts responsibility, and leaves a legacy his loved ones can proudly inherit. He's not going through the motions and bitching about the wrongs of the world. Simply not being a dick is a low bar to clear. You can do better than that. Strip away your notions of traditional manhood, whatever that even means. Masculinity for the twenty-first century leaves the door open to men of all sizes, shapes, colors, creeds, and orientations. If you are independent in spirit, bold in your actions, and compassionate in your heart—if you're ready to maximize the latter half of your life—then join us.

This book is divided into six Fs that every Midlife Male is trying to improve:

- Family (Friends)
- Fitness (Health)
- Food (Nutrition)
- Fashion (Style)
- Fun (and More Fun!)
- Finance (Money Matters)

In each of these areas, this book offers people, examples, ideas, and questions that will boost your confidence and creativity to make the rest of your life the best of your life. This book is not going to have hidden symbolism or a lot of five-syllable words that require you to whip out a dictionary to understand. I want the purpose and suggestions to be as clear as possible so that you can stop turning pages and get back to embracing your life in real time. Hell, I've even put the takeaway at the top of each chapter to speed things along for you.

I don't have all the answers, but I do know where to go for support and suggestions. I research solutions. I talk to friends and experts, including many on my weekly *Midlife Male* podcast. Think of these pages as a chance to sit in my host's chair in the studio. Sample the food, travel, clothes, and workouts that my guests and I like, laugh and share and chill with us, and see what works for you.

Just as importantly, join the Midlife Male Movement. To start with, you contribute when you are unapologetic and open. Join me as we…

- get naked (i.e., vulnerable),
- get iconic (i.e., invest in what lasts, and keep it simple),
- get curious (i.e., open yourself to new ideas and experiences),
- get moving (i.e., explore, don't decay), and most of all…
- get real.

Keep these commands in mind, and reclaiming your masculinity becomes not just attainable but a helluva lot of fun in the process. When you're vulnerable, authentic, and ready to explore, and when you invest in what matters and what lasts, you're going to like what you see when you look in the mirror.

REAL TALK

(A Disclaimer)

You're not one of those guys who buys a book that looks interesting, then puts it on his nightstand and never cracks it open. Are you? Hey, no judgment from me if you are. We've all been there. A Notes list on your phone with exercises to try, podcasts to listen to, books to read, series to watch, toys to play with—how much of it do you act on? Best-laid plans and all of that.

I'm not going to tell you this book has all the answers. I'm not a doctor, a financial planner, a psychologist, a personal trainer, or a CPA. Don't take my advice over professionals in medicine, fitness training, nutrition, money management, or other areas where you need to do your research. And don't use me as a scapegoat if you don't reach your goals.

I'm here to support you, but you've got to do the work yourself.

I have, however, lived an eventful, varied life and know many others who have as well. Some—I hope most—of this book will have value for you. Perhaps some of it won't. What I can promise you is that I'm going to be real with you. You may not agree with everything I say, but you may find you're glad I said it. Give yourself a chance to explore what works for you. You'll either take action as a result of what you read here, or you'll find an excuse not to do it. Once you've spent your $29.95, it's out of my hands.

Do us both a favor—read the book, keep it with you to refer back to now and then, take action toward maximizing your life and becoming a badass, then tell others about it.

And if you're just letting this book gather dust, gift it to somebody who will put it to good use.

The First F
FAMILY

- [ ] Are you afraid to talk to your wife when the two of you disagree?
- [ ] When was the last time you initiated an activity with your child?
- [ ] What makes your child laugh?
- [ ] If I gave you $2,000 to take your partner on a date, what would you do?
- [ ] What was the last really good gift you gave to your partner?
- [ ] Is your will taken care of?
- [ ] Do your kids know what you do to earn a living?
- [ ] If you could go into business with your spouse, would you?
- [ ] If you wrote a dating profile for your partner, what would it say?
- [ ] If your partner wrote a dating profile for you, what would it say?
- [ ] What would you tell your children on a video to be played after your death?
- [ ] When was the last time you gave your partner a compliment?
- [ ] Do you check in with your buddies, or do they check in with you?
- [ ] Do you have quality friends or quantity friends?

CHAPTER 1

Live the "Hit Life"

Focus on the long game and experiences, not one big moment.

The Hit Life is the cornerstone of my life. It applies well beyond songwriters. Finance, venture capital, real estate, school-teachers . . . society pushes us to view achievements as big milestone moments. I've seen a lot of people in the music industry get caught up in that. It makes sense: make your first million, or a number one hit, or get a car or a house. But we attach ourselves to these locations that validate the work we're doing. A lot of songwriters focus on the hit-song moment. It's a rush hearing your song on the radio over and over, there's financial windfall, it validates what you do. But that moment doesn't last long in the scheme of a person's life.

When you hit one of those milestones there's an understandable human arrogance that comes into play. You just think you'll keep repeating it over and over. All likelihood, it won't. I've witnessed a lot of really talented people I love spend their lives in pursuit of that hit-song moment—in business, it's 'I built this company and sold it'—only to find themselves on the other side of it still unhappy and unfulfilled. In years of seeing my colleagues and friends, I see that it doesn't ensure a larger secure platform of happiness.

What I'm most proud of as Pink's friend, not just as someone who has been making records with her for a long time, is that she has the Hit Life. Pink's worked incredibly hard for the life she's created for herself. What you see and what you hear in interviews or on stage, that is who she is. And the authenticity around her is what gets people so revved up and enthusiastic about her career. She says it like it is. She is who she is. We've been doing it a long time. She's been a great friend to me. She is a great philanthropist and a very devoted mother and wife. She's just an awesome person. I mean, you hear this stuff, and someone says, "Oh, so and so is so great." Anything you want to know about her in terms of "Is there depth there?" she's been open about it. She's been open about her views on women. She's been open about the challenges in her marriage. She's been open about her political views. She's authentic. In many respects, there's not a lot about her on that macro level that you don't already know. I can just validate it and tell you she is absolutely 100 percent fucking real.

I would say any healthy relationship needs that kind of transparency. You want a great marriage, you want a great business partnership, you want great friends? If you're faking any of it, then you're never going to know how real it is or how real it can be or how not real it is. It's scary for anybody to be transparent. Anybody certainly struggles with the three tiers of their lives: your outward persona, your public life. And then you have your personal life. And then you have your secret life. Nine times out of ten, that's how people function. To be able to accomplish a through line, real consistency through those three levels—it doesn't mean you have to tell your secret life to someone you just met, but it means that the level of integrity is commensurate with the level of intimacy with the people that you engage with.

> — **BILLY MANN,** songwriter, music producer, entrepreneur, philanthropist, and founder of Green & Bloom/Topline and Manncom Creative Partners, on *The Midlife Male* podcast, Episode #10

* * *

Billy Mann has worked with John Legend, Celine Dion, and many others. Listening to him share about one of the most well-known of his many musical collaborations, I couldn't help but think of an old-time newspaper headline splashed in forty-eight-point type across the top of the page:

MANN TO MEN: TO MAN UP, THINK PINK

Truly, guys, what Billy is talking about here should be seen as front-page material. If the value of getting vulnerable is news to you, then there's no time like the present to flip the script. My guess is you've heard this plenty, but it's easy for men to ignore. If life is going well, then we don't want to take time to dive deeper, to reflect on what's going on behind the success. Hell, that kind of self-awareness might ruin what has us looking good to the world! And if things are in the crapper, we sure don't want to ask for support or look for an alternative way. We might accidentally expose a weakness that someone might use against us!

Pink is a badass, but so is Billy. He's behind the scenes and just as much of a role model when it comes to practicing authenticity. And what does that kind of openness get you? It will probably get you some haters and doubters. Some people can't handle the truth. More profoundly, it will also get you friends who will go to the mat for you and whom you also will stand up for.

The Hit Life is all about quality over quantity. When you raise intimacy with others, you raise your integrity. Then the quality of your relationships goes higher and the quality of your life follows. Commitment to the Hit Life helps you avoid the traps that grown men seem to climb into when it comes to interacting with other human beings. The Hit Life is striving for more than just the plaque on the wall or a hit song's chart position or your picture on the cover of *Rolling Stone*. The Hit Life is a direction; it's in motion.

You can go for a hit song in your areas of interest in life, but don't let it deter you from the Hit Life. Keep your eye not just on the ball but on the larger experience.

Instead of setting a goal of a certain amount of money, focus on defining abundance.

Instead of bragging about your big vacation, think of how big the world is and where else would be meaningful to you.

Instead of putting up with coworkers, clients, or bosses who sap your energy, create situations where you work with people you love on collaborative projects that inspire you—where negativity and the crush of trying to take credit for success aren't going to destroy the good vibes.

The Hit Life is centered on the heart; the hit song is all about the ego.

Anybody driven enough to attain something that looks glamorous *can* get it. The question is at what cost. If you're focused on getting a million dollars or six-pack abs or a C-suite position, you can get it. You may not get anything else or develop any other discernible skills or emotions, and you may destroy people, property, and perhaps yourself in the process, but you can get it. Once you get there, don't expect to feel fundamentally different though. You're as complete or as broken as you were before you embarked on that quest.

One-hit wonders

I think a lot about one-hit wonders. They catch shit for not writing a follow-up hit song. In business, I've heard entrepreneurs say that "you only have to be right once." And that's true. I don't knock the one-hit wonder. In fact, I respect someone who has a hit, makes their money, takes their chips off the table, and moves on with their life. Start a company, sell a company, live a life. Or, if they still enjoy making music or running businesses, they keep going for it, even if they never top the charts again. I wish that good fortune on everybody. Notice I didn't say lucky. I don't think it's luck, and saying it's luck devalues the hard work people put in every day. The "lucky" have worked their asses off. There are no overnight successes.

Whatever you try to attain, go into it knowing the hit song is highly unlikely. That doesn't make you a failure. That's an unfair burden to put on yourself. That shouldn't dull your ambition, but it should help inoculate you against others' measuring sticks and timeline.

Songwriting and music may seem exotic, but they're no different than other endeavors. Whatever you do, the Hit Life is about enjoying what you're doing for hours each day, month after month, year after year—even when you're not enjoying it.

The Hit Life applies not just to your relationships with people but to your relationship with money and how you construct fun on your terms.

Are you chasing the hit single or the Hit Life?

Nineteen Reasons Why Midlife Is the Best Phase of Life

- [ ] Amazing kids. I won't tear-jerk you with my feelings here, but I sincerely hope that everyone feels the way I do about my boys and gets as much joy out of being a dad as I do.

- [ ] Experience. I never really stuck with anything earlier in life. I had a chip on my shoulder and didn't really have an identity or a mentor. I chased stuff that ultimately wasn't of interest or importance, or I just plain fucked it up and had regret. As I age, things have gotten simpler and clearer.

- [ ] Fewer fucks given—not *zero*, but fewer. Family, a few friends, solid face-to-face conversations, good health, good career, good food, a few trips a year.

- [ ] In a few years, we'll be empty nesters. Now is the best time. I don't want to miss anything!

- [ ] Sex. It's better and more consistent. Your partner is right there next to you. Be nice, initiate, date your wife, and you'll get more than most.

- [ ] Broader network, better connections.

- [ ] I'm on bonus time. My dad was forty-seven when he passed, and I've made it farther than that. I've just always wanted to make it to the second half. Live, learn, love, laugh. I'm finally just now starting to figure all that stuff out.

- I have the time to just focus on doing things better. Be a better husband and a better dad, maintain my health, improve financially, fine-tune my career, be a better friend.

- You tend to care less about what other people think and not let the noise of others' opinions drown out your inner voice. Most importantly, you have the courage to follow your heart and intuition.

- Improved power of perception.

- No pretending. You can just be yourself.

- Relationships and experiences have become more important and valuable than things.

- I've made new friends who are very different from other (old) friends.

- I have the luxury to do as I please.

- Everything still bothers me. I just handle it better . . . move on and focus on controlling what I can control.

- I've started giving more and expecting less.

- I have the conversations I want rather than engaging in the interactions I don't care for.

- I'm healthier and have more energy than I ever have.

- I spend a lot less time on my hair.

CHAPTER 2

Be the Partner Your Partner Deserves

Don't take your significant other for granted.

For forty days at the beginning of quarantine, a friend of mine, Boyd Varty, who is a South African lion tracker, decided he was going to spend forty days and forty nights on the game reserve at Londolozi, South Africa. Basically, he was going to live in a tree. It's not technically a tree house, but there was a platform, a bed, and some stuff with a tarp over it in case it rained, but he was living out on the land. Now, what was really cool about that, aside from all the obvious cool parts of it, was that Boyd would do a ten- or fifteen-minute daily broadcast. He would drop it off at a particular place, and these people would go grab it and put up the podcast. How I would start my day is I would get up, make coffee, and my wife and I would sit on our couch, and we would listen to

Boyd. I highly recommend all your listeners go to his podcast, Track Your Life with Boyd Varty. *It's forty days, and each day, he's an incredible storyteller and has a deep wisdom about him that is ageless. Each day it was just like freakin' mind-blowing what he'd come up with, to the point that we were like, 'Dude, can you just have an off day?!' It was amazing. It was a way for us to settle into our day together.*

That ends. At forty days, it's over. My wife and I sit and have our coffee and just have conversations again. That's been great. But on Saturday night, we have a guesthouse, and so we slept in the guesthouse. We had kind of a date night, and we played Scrabble and just had an awesome night, just listening to records. We woke up the next morning and I made us coffee, and I picked up The Wisdom of Insecurity, *by Alan Watts, and just picked up a random page and read it to her. I read the page, and we just started talking about it. Thirty minutes later, she picks up* The Mastery of Love, *by Don Miguel Ruiz, and randomly reads four or five pages. Not surprisingly, they intertwine, and we sit and have an hour-long conversation. It occurs to us, it would be fun to just do this as a podcast. So Monday, I set up the mics, and we just sat down and had coffee and just riffed on whatever we wanted. We'd read some stuff. Our mornings now are started with this podcast, which I may or may not release. I'll probably put it up on YouTube, and if I feel like it, it will be a podcast, but it's a way for us to have a conversation and share what we're learning or unlearning and have some fun with it and be intentional.*

Every morning we'll have a conversation and we'll record it for fun. Today was a little bit more fun than yesterday because we were like, this needs to be more like just a conver-

sation. It was a little like a podcast yesterday because that's my default. I've recorded about twenty or twenty-five podcasts by now, and that's just what I know. So today, it's like, "You cut me off whenever you want. Let's show the ten people who are 'in the room' the real us as much as you can, knowing that there are mics there." That's how we start our day.

— **CAL CALLAHAN,** entrepreneur and creator of
The Great Unlearn podcast, on *The Midlife Male*
podcast, Episode #111

* * *

You read that right. Cal just introduced an African lion tracker—a lion tracker is a thing?!—and did not make him the central part of the story. He turned Boyd's podcast into a recommendation for getting closer to your partner. I couldn't agree with him more. What's most important in life? Relationships.

You don't have to set up mics—or mood lighting or candles, for that matter—with your honey. Whatever you do, though, I highly suggest you take Cal's advice to be intentional and tap into "the real us." That's how you maximize your family, friends, and connections, which is important at any age, but especially when you've been around long enough to have experienced loss and also know who you can count on to be rock solid until the end. Define family as broadly as you like. The bottom line is you need to have people you relate to and can confide in.

This chapter is about intimate relationships. I'm not saying you should be single or in a committed situation. I realize not everyone has a life partner or even wants one. I will say that since I am in a heterosexual marriage, my examples often come from that experience. But however you identify, you have just as much right and responsibility to be miserable or happy as anyone does. Whatever your preference, the takeaways in this chapter are universal—how you show up for your partner and what you expect from them in return.

Finding my lifesaver

A committed relationship has been a game changer for me. It's not an exaggeration to say my wife has been a lifesaver. I was in my early twenties, drifting personally but masking that reality with professional success and a lot of alcohol. I had left Miramax and was living my dream of being in the film industry. I was an independent producer with a couple of films under my belt: *Two Ninas*, with Ron Livingston (yup, the guy from *Office Space*), Amanda Peet, and Cara Buono; and *Boricua's Bond*, a hip-hop movie that to this day I've still never watched.

I literally fell for Kate while in California on a trip to sell the foreign rights to these movies. Actually, I fell *over* her while drunk at the Skybar at the Mondrian Los Angeles hotel. I was a mess. To this day, I have no idea why she took pity on me and gave me a chance to talk with her again. I would never recommend this as a pickup attempt, but we did start dating. After several months of doing the long-distance thing, I convinced her to move down to South Beach, where I was then working for The Shooting Gallery (another indie film company whose claim to fame was the

Billy Bob Thornton movie *Sling Blade*) to see whether this was going to work between us.

It was a do-or-die moment for the relationship. I hadn't been in South Beach very long, so neither of us knew anybody. I wasn't partying so much once we started dating, but I was still drinking too much. It took a huge leap of faith for her to accept that invite. I was not in a good place, but she saw something in me that made her willing to take that monumental step. Even then, when I was an idiot in so many ways, I was smart enough to understand that she believed in me more than I believed in myself. If that's not a trait to hang onto, I don't know what else I can tell you, brother.

Truly, almost immediately after Kate got to Miami, I started to turn myself around. I reduced a lot of the drinking, got back into the gym, and began to regain some of my health. Within two years, The Shooting Gallery was belly-up, but Kate and I were very much in business. We took a two-week bike trip through French wine country to figure out our next move. We chose Houston. That's where she was from. I grew up in Great Neck on the north shore of Long Island—yes, Gatsby country—and had started my film career at Miramax—yes, Weinstein country; more on that later—and I knew I didn't want to go back to the New York lifestyle anymore. Kate and I were shaping our own future.

Kate, in every way imaginable, grounded me. If how she influenced me in just those first three years was impressive, just think what magic she's worked over twenty years of marriage. I can only hope that I've given her a portion of that value as a return on her investment. Kate's made me a better partner, no doubt about that. The result is that we are an incredible team that keeps getting better. Whether parenting, encouraging each other to expand our horizons, confronting our insecurities, or balancing what we can afford with what we really want and need, we are in this together. Full stop.

However, if you had told me in my twenties that I'd be married with kids and living in Houston, Texas, I would've told you, "Bet the under, it'll never happen." That's life for ya.

Take responsibility

I got lucky. I can say that with no apology, no self-deprecation, and no gloating.

I recognize that I am blessed to have found the love of my life and, just as importantly, that she accepted me, bullshit and all, and that we discovered each other early enough that we've gotten to build a long life together.

If that makes you want to tune me out, I get it. But grab your phone and take that selfie first. There will be plenty of men who are married when they pick up this book. By the time they finish it, they may not be. That's just math. Are you on the verge of being a statistic? You'll always be a parent, but you may not always be a husband. I'm here to tell you, maybe you're the problem. Try to convince me that your partner is the problem, and I'll tell you I've got another appointment I'm late for. Because even if you're right, you're wrong. You're fighting a losing war if your goal is to win the Battle of I'm Right. As for me? I'd rather you both be happy and apart than together and miserable.

These are supposed to be the best years of your life. Do what it takes to get there.

And when you're checking yourself out in that selfie, here's what you should be saying to yourself:

"Every problem I've had is my fault; every success I've had is shared."

And that goes for every endeavor you've ever had and any you're going to take on. It sure as hell includes your marriage. When you're a selfish, reckless, drunk, close-minded narcissist, you won't do well in the world. You know how I know that? Because I *was* that, for far too long. I even made it look like I was being successful going that route, but that comes with a steep price of a lot of pain and emptiness. If I had success that way, at least by society's fickle standards, then I know I could have had so much more if I had created success by standards that I defined.

Being selfish and close minded is a shitty way to play the long game. Even the drunk narrator of "Margaritaville" finds self-discovery—from "I know it's nobody's fault" to "Hell, it could be my fault" to "I know it's my own damn fault." If Jimmy Buffett can make that shift in four minutes, so can you. Self-awareness, deeper relationships, opinions that evolve . . . that's how you reach midlife knowing there's a lot of gas left in the tank and miles of roads well worth traveling on.

Believe me and say it with me again: "Every problem I've had is my fault; every success I've had is shared."

Yep.

Create a winning team

Teamwork is a common thread I hear from successful men when they talk about their spouses. If there is a lack of balance between what both partners bring to the table, the relationship can't last. Or at least it shouldn't. You're both going to have strengths and weaknesses, and if you're a strong team, you can suss that out to help each other and navigate daily life. In a sense, that's the easy stuff.

More importantly, you both have to be contributing and filling the cup of the other in an equitable way if you're going to play the long game. Emotionally, cognitively, sexually, when making important decisions, when dealing with crises, and when telling hard truths. Don't expect your partner to be all things at all times. That's not fair to them any more than it's fair for them to expect it of you. We all need our guy time, our alone time, and our coaches and confidants. But you'd sure as hell better be able to communicate clearly about when and how you need their support, when you need to seek it elsewhere, and how to respond when they ask you for your support. It's not how well you do all of this that matters as much as that you're authentically making the effort to do it, consistently and willingly.

You'll get better at it over time if your intention is clear. Trust me.

Better yet, trust your partner. They'll let you know.

Fuck Us and Feed Us

I read about a study in which one of the findings was that married women felt more in control of their sex lives than men did.

No shit . . . No married guy needs a study to tell him that. It really could have been all of two lines:

Q: "What makes men happy?"

A: "Fuck us and feed us." End of study.

Guys aren't really that complex. Fuck and feed us and you'll get pretty much anything you want. I don't know any guy who is getting laid and eating well who isn't happy.

That may sound a little old school, but I know you know what I'm saying. I totally own being very simple to figure out—don't think I didn't consider making this page the seventh F. Instead, that seventh F is G rated and will come later (but I did manage to slide this by the editor and get it in).

Still, there is more to say about this subject. Be a caring man, but don't be a pushover either. Confidence helps protect against this. It's not just you being the type of partner your partner deserves; it's you being the type of partner that *you* deserve.

This isn't just about not getting run over; it's also about not being a victim and venting to your buddies about how awful your wife is. If that's how you deal with your problems, the problem isn't your wife.

Pick your spots. Be on equal ground. Respect your partner, and expect to receive respect in return. Then you've got a great situation. Lopsided never works. If you're initiating 90 percent of the time, that's not good. If you're giving in 90 percent of the time, that isn't good either.

I've got a suggestion for how you and your partner can make those numbers align better. Bet you can guess which two rooms they involve.

CHAPTER 3
Father Up

Make sure your family will be taken care of financially and emotionally when you're gone.

I was in south Texas on a business trip and got in a horrific car accident on the freeway. In the middle of the crushing metal and the breaking glass and me consuming an airbag in my face, I thought, I'm going to die, and who is going to raise my sons? There's no question that my wife Erica is an amazing mom and would do a phenomenal job of teaching them the things they need to know, but at that moment I felt cheated out of being a dad and passing on the things that I believed I needed to share with my boys. But I walked away from this accident with a bruised hip and a totaled rental car. About an hour later, I'm sitting in my hotel room with the shakes, and I picked up my computer and created a file for my sons called If Anything Ever Happens To Me. In that file,

I just started adding instructions to life and people I'd like them to meet. And life lessons I had experienced but hadn't shared with them yet.

One of the things I believe is that everybody needs a good mentor. So I went to my mentor and said to him, "If anything ever happens to me, can you please pass on what you've shared with me and take on that responsibility and pass it on to my sons." He just said, "What are you talking about?!" I told him how I created this file for my boys, and he said, "I'd like to see this file." I gave him access to it online, and he came back a couple days later and said, "Jonathan, I just don't think this is a file for your boys." And I thought I'd missed the mark somehow. I really respected this man's opinion and approach and how he instructed me. I said, "Wow, what did I do wrong?" He goes, "You haven't done anything wrong. You're thinking too small. This isn't a file for your boys. There's a kid down the street from me who needs this file. He needs to learn what you're teaching your sons in this. I have a grandson who needs to learn this. There are boys everywhere that have gaps in their life who aren't being taught the skills and character traits they need to succeed. This isn't a file for your boys. This is a book." It took me about a minute of talking to my wife, and off we launched. It's for people asking, "How do you launch boys into men?"

— **JONATHAN CATHERMAN,** bestselling author and
founder/director of the 1M Mentoring Foundation,
on *The Midlife Male* podcast, Episode #141

* * *

The Manual to Manhood and subsequent books that Jonathan and Erica have written are not just about launching boys into manhood. They're also about being a father who raises empowered daughters who see how men should treat women in intimate relationships, friendships, and the workplace. They're about becoming a mentor and instilling confidence in youth no matter who they are. As Jonathan said, "Everybody needs a good mentor."

Losing my first—and best—mentor

As I write this, I'm forty-nine years, two months, and two days old—or as I like to say, I'm 429 days into bonus time.

My boys are now eighteen and fifteen. It's hard to fathom what it would be like if I died now. I don't want to miss out on a single minute of their lives—seeing what they'll get passionate about and how their views of the world will evolve, meeting hypothetical daughters-in-law and grandchildren, following them as they make whatever mark they leave on the world, which of course is going to be amazing, said the proud father. It would suck to be gone before I experience more of that. Not just for me, but for them.

I know because I was about my sons' age, seventeen, when my father passed away. I still feel that loss daily. He was forty-seven years old, so my forty-eighth birthday was emotional for me. Because of his death, my perspective as I became an adult has always been that I should live life to the fullest and that anything beyond forty-seven would be bonus time. Well, here I am, and if I was living large *then*, you should see me *now*.

It doesn't mean I'm climbing Everest—though I did recently do a thirty-mile hike through Utah mountains. I pick three physical challenges for myself every year, but you don't have to take part in some massive event to ensure you're living a full life. I'm not sailing around the world or betting the deed to my house on a Vegas weekend—but if you have the means and the stomach for either of those, more power to you.

Actually, playing with house money to me isn't necessarily about going bigger; it's about knowing where it is worth spending my limited resources—time, energy, and money—and prioritizing those things to create the life I choose. What that means to me in practice is that I invest in what I believe, make time for my wife and boys every day, compete in athletic and physical challenges, and do a podcast and newsletter every week. There's a lot more I do and plenty more I can't wait to try.

I am adventurous, but I'm also more aware of the importance of being responsible than ever before. At midlife, staying active and being responsible are dual priorities you have to take seriously.

My dad took care of his business, so before he ever got ill with cancer at age forty-four, he made sure we would be taken care of when he died. That's a man for you, people. He was my closest friend and confidant when I was growing up. Within weeks of me leaving for my freshman year of college, he was gone. My mom and my two brothers, ages fourteen and eight, had a whole new world to navigate. When loved ones die, it has a major impact on your psyche. It was almost thirty years ago, and I remember it like it was yesterday. I was in the room when he died, holding his hand.

It's not about you anymore

The fact is, most of us will miss a lot of our kids' movies. I certainly hope I miss the *ends* of my boys' movies. That's OK. That's natural. It's sure as hell better than the alternative—burying your child. What's important is to make the most of the time you have with your kids, whether you're gone in the first act or halfway through the third.

Bob Dylan sang, "It's not dark yet, but it's gettin' there." May sound morbid, but as usual, Dylan is on the right track. Don't wait for a wake-up call like Jonathan Casterman's. When it goes dark for you, make sure your children and their children will reap the benefits.

It's not about you anymore, and not just in the ways we often think about—changing diapers, answering middle-of-the-night wake-up calls, getting them from point A to point B in the time you used to do your workout, giving up last-minute weekend trips when your wife finds a killer airline deal. Maybe you've blended families from multiple marriages and are navigating the stepparent journey with your current partner. I've had friends tell me that if you're a Black man, you have to prepare your children for dealing with cops and other figures of authority.

You could have lots thrown at you that you have no control over. You may be taking care of your parents. What if your child is gay or transgender? Will you be supportive? Will you worry about prejudices they will face?

Never forget the lives that have been placed in your hands. Be grateful you've gotten that. If you're not there yet, just know you can be as prepared as possible and it still won't be enough. If you don't have kids and never plan to, take care of your business and don't be *that* guy. See the earlier section about taking responsibility.

If you don't have kids and know you never will, this chapter may seem like it isn't addressed to you. I get that, and I hope you will permit me to make a suggestion: consider ways you can make a difference in a child's life while also enjoying the opportunity to experience youthful energy. Perhaps as a mentor, foster or adoptive parent, coach, or involved uncle.

We hear all the time about how important it is to "man up" when the game is on the line or you need to make it through adversity or come through for a friend in need. All true. Equally as important is making sure you "father up." Because your kids are the most important people in your life who at some point—guaranteed—will need some help when the game is on the line (whether they made or missed the buzzer-beater), when they go through a tough time (hint: you don't have to solve it for them), or when they are in need (emotionally, for sure; maybe at times financially. What's your plan for that conversation, Dad?).

Up your father game immediately, because these kids you brought into the world didn't ask for you and won't always ask for help, but they *need* you. In some ways, fathering is the most important game you'll ever play. Contrary to what you may have been told or had modeled for you, your evolutionary duty doesn't end when you let millions of your boys swim with abandon, and your responsibility as a father isn't just making sure there's food on the table.

Excel as a father the entire time your kids are on this planet, and leave them a legacy to strive for when you're gone. *Then* you've done your job. The rest of life is gravy.

Maxims for the Discerning MLM

There is still peer pressure at forty-six.

Numbers don't lie.

You have nobody to blame but yourself.

Your attitude is a choice.

The amount of effort you put into something is 100 percent up to you.

It takes as much work to do something small as it does to go big.

Everybody wants something.

Set boundaries.

Discipline equals freedom.

If you ignore your reality, you can't get ahead.

Trying is not doing.

#MidlifeMale
#BeYou

CHAPTER 4

Are You a Dad or a Parent?

Be present with your family.
Learn to combine fun and discipline.

Because of the relationship and trust KD and I formed as friends, as family, and because of the respect he has for the work I do and the love I have for both sides of what we do— the business and him—we really have the most fair relationship. I'm always going to pick up the phone for him, but he doesn't need to always call me. We talk about everything, and there's some things he really wants to interject and have an opinion on, some things he trusts me, some things he wants to put to bed, and other things that are just his, not just from a business standpoint but that he wants to build and ideate on. The things that he needs in his life, I've been doing for so long that the relationships that I have with his family and

49

the people that work for him are no different than how I'd talk with my own family. I'm somebody that relishes that role. I like taking care of people, and I'm comfortable taking care of people. I care about him, but because of that, it seamlessly fits. He cares about my wife and kids and understands that I'm a family man first and foremost. Kevin's a grown man. He doesn't need me.

I check the boxes of a good dad in every sense of the word. I'm present, I love them unconditionally, I believe in them, I'm honest with them, I have them be honest with me. But at the same time, I don't think it's fair to necessarily judge the kind of dad I am based on the boxes that people think ought to be checked, because I think there's a lot of things I could improve upon as a dad that there aren't boxes for. I would do anything for them, and they know that. They're honest with me—or I think they're honest with me. The things that I could do better are more internal, and I'm always thinking about that. I'm aware of it now more than ever because the things I'm experiencing as a dad, they're not going to remember the same way. Those moments are just mine, and my wife's to some extent, and my own thoughts—like, what did I not do there, or how much did I miss when they were a baby?

My memories from childhood are from, like, eight to eighteen. That's where my parents fucked me up in my mind. That's where they did shit wrong. That's where I can consciously remember the things that went wrong. When my parents hear me say it, they'll say to me we had amazing times. They're going to reference times I'll never ever remember. So what I think about now is that yeah, I'm there and I'm doing the right things, but how am I reacting to you, or how lazy am I being on Saturday and projecting that onto you?

I remember as a kid being like, why the fuck are my parents fighting right now, or why the hell is my dad telling me, "Get off your ass!" That's the thinking in my head.

The day-to-day things, I've gotta make these moments, I gotta make these memories. I've got to do better. I've gotta take serious what my kid is going through with a group of friends because at age ten that was real shit. I can't be like, "Oh, stop that shit." To a kid, the stakes are everything. The next level, which I'm really trying to get to, is to make the next few years about what they want to do. Really consciously thinking about it. And there's not much time left. My kids are eleven and seven.

But I have to be reminded of it. My wife said today, "It's supposed to be nice on Saturday. Let's go to Rye Playland." This was my answer: "You know I hate roller coasters and shit." That has nothing to do with me though. That instinct has to get better. I want them to hold those moments.

— **RICH KLEIMAN,** cofounder and partner of Thirty Five Ventures and The Boardroom with Kevin Durant, on *The Midlife Male* podcast, Episode #142

* * *

I've known Rich since Camp Winaukee in Center Harbor, New Hampshire, from the time we were seven through thirteen. Those were some days: play, swim, eat; play, swim, eat, sleep; and repeat for eight weeks. He's been managing Kevin Durant for years and now is business partners with him. Before that he was vice president of sports at Jay-Z's Roc Nation. He's not lacking in confidence is what I'm saying.

I can totally relate to his intentions and insecurities when it comes to raising kids. Each day, I wonder if I'm doing my part in passing along the life skills and traits to my sons that will make them confident and prepared. Each day. In recent years, I've reconnected with him—one of the joys of middle age, by the way, seeing what friends and acquaintances have been up to for the past thirty years. I know how seriously he takes fatherhood.

I'm guessing you can relate to Rich and me too, no matter how good or bad of a job you think you're doing. You're doing your best, and sometimes your best is Dad of the Year material. Sometimes it's shit. You let your ego or your own stressors swirl around in your head and spew out of your mouth if you're not grounded and considering what your family needs. Don't beat yourself up over it. You're not going to bat 1.000 on this. Shoot, stay above the Mendoza Line, and you may be in all-star territory when it comes to being a parent.

Be engaged, and be willing to apologize and even laugh about it when you mess up. And when you are engaged, you are in the best position to contribute a father's perspective and make sure your values are heard. I'm sure your wife is calling a lot of the shots, as she should, but all families benefit when fathers step up and take the lead some of the time. You will make an impression if you take the lead, not just when it comes to having fun but by being real. That's where leading by example actually comes from. I want to be my sons' best friend, but they need a parent first. Don't misunderstand me. I'm friends with my sons, but the bigger responsibility and obligation is raising good men.

I look at being a dad and being a parent as two separate parts of my job. The dad stuff is joking, playing, talking, cuddling, sports, traveling, experiencing things together. The parenting stuff is the discipline, homework, responsibilities, finances, scheduling, life lessons. For me, the fun is easy, and the accountability is hard. For you, it might be the opposite.

Both parenting and being a dad are important, but the key is not to slack off on the one that is more difficult. I don't want to be a "Do as I say, not as I do" kind of guy. That creates a constant struggle between authenticity and hypocrisy. If you're not leading by example, what kind of message are you sending?

- What message are we sending if we come home drunk from a party and our kids see it? (They can tell, even if we convince ourselves that they can't.) Or if we're visibly intoxicated at a party in front of our kids?

- What message are we sending if we want our kids to be athletic, active, and in shape but we're not doing anything physical ourselves?

- What message are we sending if we allow our kids to exclude others because we don't want them to deal with their own insecurities or challenges?

- What message are we sending if we choose to blame teachers, coaches, and volunteers and seek to change classes or teams for our kids rather than teaching them accountability by handling adversity without our interference or assistance?

- What message are we sending if we talk on the phone or text while driving and then tell our kids to never talk or text in the car?
- What message are we sending if we lie, avoid, or manipulate the truth and then expect our kids to be honest and trustworthy with us?
- What message are we sending if we secretly smoke or do drugs and then tell our kids how bad smoking and drugs are for them? Again, they can tell, even if we convince ourselves that they can't.

The actions (or lack thereof) we take on a daily basis, big or small, make lasting impressions. I'm going to make mistakes. My kids are too. But they need to know we're figuring it out together.

Eighteen and Life to Go, from Your Father

I'm not sure when I started to put this list together, but I just started compiling things I've read that resonated, personal experiences I wanted to pass along, and quotes or sayings that made an impact.

1. You are loved. Every minute of every day, no matter what, I love you.
2. I am always there for you. Any time, any place, and at any moment. You call on me and I am there.
3. I will not wait for you to reach out to me. I will always be reaching out to you. This may annoy you at times. One day, when you have a child, you'll understand.
4. You are never too old to need your dad.

5. You weren't born to fit in, conform, or go along to get along. You don't have to. You just do *you* the very best that you can.

6. Be proud of the person you are becoming.

7. Keep your mindset evolving.

8. If you don't believe in yourself, no one will do it for you.

9. Quality over quantity. This is applicable with women, friends, business associates, clothing, food, money, fitness . . . everything.

10. Always respect women. Take your time to find the right one.

11. Take the initiative. You'll never regret going after what you want.

12. Always acknowledge and reciprocate.

13. Simplicity is the end result of long, hard work, not the starting point.

14. Getting anywhere great in life has less to do with how right you are and more to do with the ability to recognize where you're wrong.

15. Never allow someone else to dictate the outcome of your life.

16. Learn how to say *no.* Saying no effectively gives you the opportunity and availability to say yes to what you really want to do.

17. Look for activities, people, jobs, experiences that fill your tank, not empty it. Negativity is a cancer.

18. Apologize when you're wrong. "I'm sorry" goes a long way.

19. Apologize even when you feel you're right. "I'm sorry you feel that way" goes a long way as well.

20. Keep your eyes, ears, and heart open to what feels good, authentic, purposeful, and brings you joy and contentment. Happiness comes from within.

21. Know who you are. This will take time, and you will change. Your mother is one of the most remarkable people when it comes to this. She knows exactly who she is. She's not right as often as she thinks, ha . . . but she's never in doubt. Learn from her.

22. Confidence is a skill. Skills take practice. Work on your confidence. Experiment with what makes you feel secure, empowered, on top of your game, and strong. When you find it, embrace it and use it.

23. Get comfortable being uncomfortable. Life will throw all sorts of situations at you. A lot of them are going to suck. It's all about how you handle it.

24. Get comfortable being comfortable. Not everything needs to be pushed to extremes. Sometimes, being comfortable is more than enough.

25. People don't always remember what you say, but they always remember how you make them feel.

26. Work on both your weaknesses and your strengths. There will be things you're not good at that you'll need to get good at, things that you're not good at that are a waste of time trying to get good at, and things that you're good at that you should spend time getting great at!

27. ROL is more important that ROI—think return on life, not just return on investment. Focus on the bigger picture, and you'll have a much greater overall return.

28. You don't want to die with your sailboat still in your driveway. Coffins don't have pockets. Take the trip or the gap year, and have as many experiences as you can. No regrets.

29. Ask for help. No one accomplishes anything on their own.

30. Your company doesn't care about you. Pay attention here. There's *nothing* wrong with working for a company. Learn, understand, and navigate to the best of your advantage.

31. Experiences over things. When acquiring things, look for those that create and improve your experiences.

32. Be prideful. Take pride in everything you do. Not because someone is watching (though someone always is) but because it matters to you. Ask yourself, "Am I proud of this?"

33. Also know that I am always proud of you but will call you out when you are not acting in a manner you can be proud of.

34. New goals always require new habits.

35. Discipline equals freedom. It took me a long time to realize and implement this one. If you want to have free time, open space, health, wealth, wellness, less anxiety and stress, and the opportunity to live more freely, create a routine, habits, and the discipline to have it. It's 100 percent within your control.

36. You come first. Not to be selfish, greedy, or arrogant, but you are the CEO of your own life. Run it the way you want to.

37. Money matters. Develop a relationship with it, and make choices based around the financial needs you have determined the life you want to live requires.

38. Everyone's measure of success is different. You decide what success means to you.

39. Find good mentors, advisors, men and women that you respect, and learn everything you can from them. They can be older, younger, the same age—there's always something to be learned.

40. It's OK to be a late bloomer or an early overachiever. There's no one set way to "make it."

41. That being said, life is a marathon, not a sprint. Don't rush.

42. Family comes first. These are the people who will always be there for you. You can't choose them, they may not be perfect, and you may not even always like them all, but they're yours and you are theirs. Embrace their positive attributes, and accept their flaws and shortcomings—you have your own as well.

43. Without your health you have nothing. What's the point of having an amazing family if you smoke yourself to an early death? What's the point of having a lot of money if you're too sick to enjoy it? Take care of your body and your mind. That's all you've got.

44. Live freely though. You can do everything right and still get hit by a bus. Eat the cheeseburger when you want it.

45. Finance: What's the point of having a great family, great health, and no money to enjoy life with? It matters. Put yourself in positions to earn, achieve, save, and spend wisely.

46. Food (nutrition): The world is full of flavors. Experience them. You will grow mentally, physically, spiritually, and emotionally by being open to diverse tastes. (P.S. This mindset goes for many other things as well.)

47. Fashion (style): Find clothing and a personal style that make you feel confident, authentic, and alive.

48. Fun: Don't forget to have fun. There's a difference between good fun and bad fun. Have as much good fun as you can. The consequences of bad fun can hang over you for the rest of your life.

49. Call your dad. You have a question? You're not sure about something? Worried, scared, something great happened? Call, call, call! I'll answer.

50. If you want to be appreciated, then appreciate.

51. If you wish to be respected, then respect.

52. If you wish to be loved, then love.

53. Nobody really knows anything, and certainly nobody knows everything. We're all just doing the best we can.

54. Very little is black and white. Find your place within the gray.

55. Don't participate in every fight you get invited to.

56. If and when you have to fight, strike first, strike hard, and do whatever you need to do to get home safely.

57. Learn to take care of yourself. Physically, financially, spiritually.

58. Trust but verify. Lead with trust, but once someone violates your trust, move on.

59. Forgive, but don't forget. This one is thrown around a lot. It's true. Don't carry the anger. Don't live in the past. File it, remember, learn from the experience.

60. Be kind.

61. Leave things better than you found them.

62. Don't allow anyone to mistake your kindness for weakness.

63. It takes a lot of complicated work, time, and effort to make anything look simple.

64. Keep it simple: Do the work. Measure results. Course correct. Repeat.

65. When you're serious about something, you just do it.

66. Have situational awareness. Know your surroundings, don't be distracted, don't be a target.

67. Look people in the eye.

68. Give people a second chance, but not a third.

69. Loosen up. Relax. Except for life-and-death matters, nothing is as important as it first seems.

70. Put down the phone and be present.

71. Be a good loser and a good winner.

72. Be bold and courageous. When you look back at life, you'll regret the things you didn't do more than the ones you did.

73. Take the scenic route.

74. Send lots of cards, thank-you notes, and gifts.

75. Cultivate a capacity for awareness.

76. Don't worry about what others think of you.

77. Learn to listen deeply.

78. Be responsible for your own actions, first and always.

79. Honor your word.

80. Read—all the time.

81. Learn to filter. Before you say anything, think about how the words you plan to use will sound in the ears of the person you are speaking to.

82. Learn to disagree with someone without taking personal offense, if for no reason other than that you can't expect something from someone that you aren't able to deliver yourself.

83. Learn empathy. In all situations be able to put yourself in the position of the person you're interacting with.

84. Character counts.

85. Honesty matters.

86. Stay focused and determined, and complete things.

87. Attitude is everything.

88. Be generous.

89. Never give up.

90. No one is going to do the work for you.

91. Keep a healthy balance.

92. Surround yourself with great people.

93. Take things one step at a time and everything else will fall into place.

94. Never make an important decision on an empty stomach or before you've worked out.

95. Respect other points of view.

96. You don't have to be great to start, but you do have to start to be great.

97. You don't stop playing because you get old. You get old because you stop playing.

98. No reward without the risk. You miss 100 percent of the shots you don't take.

99. Age doesn't make you a man. Actions do.

100. See #1.

Love,

Dad

Family Is My "Why"

I sometimes get tired of hearing about the importance of finding my "why."

But you know what? If you want to know the answer to everything I choose to do or not do, it's right here: My family is my "why."

I like this definition of family:

- Family provides love, support, and a framework of values to each of its members.

- Family members teach each other, serve one another, and share life's joys and sorrows.

- Families provide a setting for personal growth.

- Family is the single most important influence in a child's life.

#Family #MidlifeMale #priorities #loyalty #familyunit #trust #growth #support #health #mindset #together

CHAPTER 5

Why I Won't Be Coaching
My Son Anymore

Support your kids' activities without overtaking the activities.

I was at the Frio River. It was low, so I found this deep pocket of water and just sat in it with that cool spring water. There was a rope swing right across the river from me. For two hours I watched kids go off that rope swing, and they didn't care if they slipped off the rope early or if they went in feet-first or headfirst or if they didn't twist enough. They'd come up, huge smile on their face, and swim to the bank, get out, and do it again. I just watched them and said, "Where do kids lose that? Where do they lose that spontaneity, that flow, that fun, and that 'I don't care if I look stupid and make mistakes'? Where do they lose that in our sports culture today?" When I was growing up, we didn't worry so much about making mistakes and looking stupid. If we fell, we got up and did something harder or better. In our practice we see so many kids who are perfectionists now. They never meet their full potential because they're so afraid of upsetting parents or coaches or letting down teammates or looking stupid or being the one on that video that gets shown over and over again. We're creating an epidemic of perfectionistic athletes. We've got to do something to change that, because we're seeing kids with horrible anxiety and panic attacks.

[In organized sports], a lot of coaches let their parents make decisions or influence. I call it "protect your castle." Too many coaches have all the drawbridges down, and there's no water in the moat and no alligators, and people just come and go. You have to set up real clear parameters about what your expectations are, and if parents are out of line with that, there has to be accountability.

These parents, so many of them—not all—but they're just loose cannons. They tee off on their kids with you there. Years ago, my son was playing on a team, and we had to fire the coach because he was so brutal to our kids. Another dad took over, and he was a fireman, and he brought all his firemen to practice one day. The kids were just having a blast. All the firemen are hitting infield practice with the kids, and they're having so much fun. They got a call, and they all jump on their fire trucks and leave. Old dad takes over, and within five minutes he has the second baseman crying. The same old thing. So I walk over to the mound and I say, "You know, we ran you off a few months ago because of the way you're treating the kids, and now here you are doing it again. You're at a real important crossroads. Do you want to do things like you used to, or do you want to do it the way we want you to do *it?" He threw his glove down and said, "It's on. C'mon," and dropped an f-bomb with me in front of twelve-year-old kids. I said, "Do you really want to fight me in front of these kids?" He picked up his glove and stormed off the field—took his kid and another kid and another dad. They left the team.*

— ROBERT ANDREWS, founder, Institute of Sports Performance, and author of *Champion's Mental Edge*, on *The Midlife Male* podcast, Episode #31

* * *

If our youth are misbehaving, they're taking their cues from you. When kids are part of a team or trying out moves on the skateboard or any other physical activity, they want to have fun and maybe learn some skills. Your job as dad and/or coach isn't to prep them for the NFL Combine or push them for a full-ride scholarship. Your job is to create an environment where they will come back to that activity anytime they choose for the rest of their lives. If they learn how to do a crossover, approach, or backhand along the way, that's a bonus.

Now before you start thinking I'm going to hate on organized sports, that's not going to happen. I love the benefits that sports and physical activity provide when practiced with common sense and good intentions.

I have always enjoyed coaching my own boys, and I have enjoyed coaching other boys. I coached for ten years—that's more than a fifth of my entire life. I've made some great friends. Lost some too. I've had great experiences and made memories of a lifetime. Been a part of some big wins and some crushing defeats. And I ate a lot of shit along the way.

Most importantly, though, my decision to coach and ultimately not coach wasn't just about me. It was about coming to terms with what's best for my family, my boys, my wife, my career, and then finally . . . me.

And as much as I enjoyed coaching, I've enjoyed not coaching as well.

Sports = Fun. Full stop.

So why did I stop? For one, it just wasn't as much fun as it used to be. Simple as that. When something stops being fun, then I'm done. Above all, sports and training should be fun! Every practice and every game. For everyone . . . the parent, the child, the player, the coach. If it's not, then you should do something else.

I spent time in Steamboat, Colorado, once when my son was playing in a baseball tournament. On that particular team, I had no coaching responsibilities. I had more fun watching and supporting that team than I'd had as a coach in quite some time.

I was relaxed. I was encouraging. I was not wound up. (Perhaps it was the edibles; it was Colorado, after all. But I digress.) My wife and I got along better. My son and I got along better. He felt no pressure from me, and I felt none from him. He liked it better. I was not responsible for any crying kids—my own nor anyone else's.

I was able to go off and do my own thing, go to the games and practices I wanted to, and skip everything else. I didn't take crap from any parents. There were no schedules to coordinate, no emails to answer, and no worrying about trying to please anyone. No three-hour postgame conversations second-guessing and coulda, woulda, shoulda scenarios. I got to sleep in.

It was fucking awesome.

Tips to be the coach your kid deserves

I'm not trying to discourage you from coaching, either. Everybody's schedules are so busy anymore that youth sports leagues have trouble finding volunteer referees, umpires, and coaches. You can make a positive difference in young lives and realize some benefits yourself if you choose to make that commitment.

Do's

- Do remind your players in direct and subtle ways that they are gaining a lot out of sports—a healthy body and a chance to perform at their best, build resilience, and be leaders and good teammates. It's all about developing healthy habits early.

- Do have enough self-awareness to know that these kids don't deserve to be ground zero for your stress management. We all have stress in our lives, but for the ninety minutes you're in charge of them, you owe it to them to push your issues aside.

- Do be the parent who is willing to forgo the all-star game or the travel team in favor of a family vacation or summer camp. Your FOMO doesn't have to get transferred to the next generation. And just because your kid goes to prom doesn't mean they'll drop into the next round of the pro draft. Trust me: your kid's spot in the draft—at his or her barstool of choice watching it on TV ten years from now—is safe.

- Do be the dad who still takes care of himself physically. That way, you can play the sports your kids are playing, and you'll empathize with how difficult it is to perform the skills.

- Do be the parent or coach who instills confidence and lessens anxiety in kids by encouraging them to work hard and have fun. Kids beat themselves up mentally way too much. Maybe you do too. I've been there. But negative self-talk is the worst thing any of us can do to our self-worth and our ability to achieve goals. You can model a much different approach for the kids who look up to you.

- Do be that parent or coach who can laugh at mistakes you made. You don't have to be perfect in your words and actions. You just need to learn from them. Pro tip though: brush up on the Golden Rule if you want to be less likely to make massive mistakes.

Don'ts

- Don't be the coach who lets parents hover at practice. Maybe they need to be there because it's not practical to do the drop-off and go back home. That doesn't mean they get to make suggestions (helpful or otherwise), side-coach Junior, or roll their eyes at your drill or position selections. Your players will appreciate your zero tolerance because they will feel looser and not be looking over their shoulders.

- Don't make the sport win at all costs. Players can develop a competitive spirit without thinking the world will end if they don't get the top seed in the tournament.

- Don't push your kid or other kids to specialize in a sport until they've tried out a lot of them and it's their choice to do so. The only thing the trend toward one-sport stars creates is overuse injuries and unrealistic expectations. Being athletic for life is far more practical than being a specialist for a couple of years.

- Don't call six-year-olds *athletes*. They're not. We've already got a name for them: *kids*.

- Don't use exercise as a punishment. It's a privilege.

- Don't be the parent or coach who asks your kid why he stranded five runners on base while Johnny went three for three and made a diving catch. Your kid saw the game; he doesn't need a postgame comparative analysis.

- Don't treat every mistake or lack of ability as a physical problem to be corrected. Often, people have trouble mastering skills because of anxiety that you may be helping create. Also, maybe your kid just sucks. If they're trying and having fun, that's all that matters. You don't have to hire a bio-mechanist or a shooting coach to get them on track.

Living vicariously through your kids

Do your family a favor and stop trying to be cool. You don't need to yell at them for striking out in front of all their friends or remind them of the note they missed on the drive home from the recital. You don't need to tell the referee he missed the foul committed against your flesh and blood. I can't stand it when fathers try to live vicariously through their kids.

If you want to lift weights with your buddies or play in a band—both of which I do—or do any of a hundred other activities, then I support you 100 percent. I see that as my kids living vicariously through me, not by feeling pressured to do what I do but by seeing I'm staying active and enjoying life. Don't expect your kids to like what you want or reach whatever level of success you have outlined for them to follow. I'm not weighing in about Earl and Tiger Woods; Richard, Venus, and Serena Williams; or Marv and Todd Marinovich. Whatever good or bad you think of those dads' methods, intentions, or results, those are extreme examples. Support your kids in doing what they like to do and you'll be in a good place.

I've heard that when Bruce Springsteen showed his kids the 1980s video for "Dancing in the Dark," they just shrugged their shoulders. If The Boss can't impress his children looking like he did in jeans and a short-sleeved shirt in his thirties dancing with Courteney Cox, you don't stand a chance no matter what you do.

No regrets

I have no regrets at having stopped coaching my kids. Being part of their team experience gave me some amazing and memorable experiences. But my stepping back allowed my sons to have their own experiences with new and different coaches, which allowed them to grow as people and athletes—and allowed me to grow as a dad.

I'm grateful for all of the opportunities I've had as a coach and to the leagues and parents that supported me. I love the kids and respect the other great coaches/dads I coached with and against. I even liked most of the parents.

But . . . at some point I didn't need it anymore.

And more importantly, my sons didn't need me to coach them anymore.

They just need me to love them.

An Attitude Aid for Your Morning Routine

I picked up a little trick or attitude aid during the pandemic year of 2020. I made it a habit each morning to write down three things I'm grateful for. I still miss quite a few days, but I always feel better on the days when I write something down.

Perception and perspective really are quite amazing attributes.

These do not have to be gargantuan, life-changing things.

They can be as simple as eating a good piece of fruit (no idea why I chose that as an example) or having sex with your wife when you didn't expect it (that's a much better example).

Jot it down on a napkin while having breakfast or on your phone. I like to use my personal stationery so it's got my name on the top, and then I write a one, two, and three on the card and fill it in before I head out for the day or lock into my to-dos. This way I can keep the cards and refer to them or hand a seemingly appropriate one to my two boys when they may need a slight attitude adjustment.

CHAPTER 6

Once I Stopped Judging, I Realized How Judgmental People Are

**Criticizing others (and yourself) stunts
your personal growth.**

*I didn't go to school. I didn't study any of this shit. I didn't
go to culinary school. I certainly didn't go to business school.
I had to learn this shit from the streets. That's true. That's
where I came from. I don't necessarily recommend it for everyone. I would have loved to have had a mentor, somebody
to guide me in those early years and say, "Hey, dumbass,
you need to take a couple courses and at least understand
Business 101." That would have saved me some grief and
some effort. But I think for me, I look back and I personally*

wouldn't want that any other way. I enjoy coming up through the school of hard knocks, as they would say.

But techniques for dealing with the organized chaos at work? I don't have a technique for that. I deal with shit that comes in. I try to handle them as cool and calmly and collectively as I possibly can. I wasn't always like that. When I was younger, I was more inexperienced and handled shit more irrationally, just like most of us do. We tend to panic. I try to stay a lot more calm now. What do they say? Don't sweat the small shit.

My number one outlet—and if anyone knew me three years ago, they're not going to believe what they're hearing right now—for me is on the fitness side. Going to the gym, working out, maintaining a routine and structure and regimen. I love to make fun of everyone, but more importantly, the person I make the most fun of is myself. I used to make fun of everyone walking around in casual workout clothes. Now, I'm one of those fucking people. Any chance my wife and I have to get comfortable in joggers or whatever, we do.

— **KEN BRIDGE,** founder and CEO of Delicious Concepts and ROOVY, on *The Midlife Male* podcast, Episode #113

* * *

Ken makes a good point through a silly subject: be careful what you make fun of; someday it could be you.

"There but for the grace of God go I" is the more serious way to say it, I suppose. What comes to mind for me is Monty Python's *Life of Brian* when John Cleese, as the religious leader presiding over the stoning ceremony, chastises a guy for prematurely throwing a stone at the condemned. Cleese then gets pummeled by a hailstorm of stones thrown by the mob when he accidentally utters, "Jehovah."

But maybe that's just me.

Judging others makes it easy to close yourself off to what others are trying to tell you. Maybe you should have paid attention to what you were judging five years earlier. Maybe that IPO wasn't as doomed as you said it was when your friend tried to get you in on it at the beginning. Maybe sometimes the idiot is you. And if that's the case, acknowledge it, laugh about it, and move on.

I've been very slow to realize how judgy I can be. Big things, little things, they all get to me. I wish they didn't, but they do. It's something I work on constantly. From the demoralizing tragedies in the world (senseless mass shootings of innocent people at schools, places of worship, and workplaces) to the emotional (my kids dealing with interpersonal issues at school) to the personal (my hamstring hurting; an underwriter pulling a quote I was counting on) to other people being assholes (somebody making an illegal U-turn or cutting in line) . . . there's a shitload of things to pass judgment about.

My friend Taylor Somerville wrote on his blog, *The Long Game*, "I used to struggle with giving people the benefit of the doubt. I would typically assume the worst, that someone was acting out of malice or maybe they were lazy. Over the years, I realized this is not the best mindset to have because it only adds stress to your life, which none of us really need. Why can we be so quick to judge others? Why do we hold them to the same standards we hold ourselves?"

He's right.

I had a dad write to me in response to a decision I had made that he clearly did not agree with. He said, "The only logical explanation I can come up with is that you must be threatened by me in order to do this." He then went on to tell me all about the various things going on in his life and making judgment after judgment and assumption after assumption about mine. Never once asking, only telling.

Once I began to stop judging people, I realized just how much people judge one another. What I can confirm about worrying about what other people think is that nobody really cares about the things you're worried about or the "why" behind your decisions; they only really care about themselves and how it affects them.

Gary Vee put out a great quote that said, "Ninety-nine-point-nine percent of people that judge you or have opinions on you have no idea what the fuck is actually happening in your life."

What happens when you stop judging and making assumptions is that you free up a lot of mental, physical, and emotional capacity. I never realized how draining passing judgment is until I made a conscious effort to stop doing it!

"Be strict with yourself but forgiving of others" (another gem from Taylor). It's true. By letting go, moving on, not fighting every little thing and taking control of that which only *you* can control, you experience less stress, less anxiety, and less pressure, and conversely gain more energy, more positivity, and more time to focus on the things and people that you actually do give a fuck about.

"Be strict with yourself but forgiving of others."

—TAYLOR SOMERVILLE

* * *

Judging others is a quick way to end up alone. So is allowing the judgment and opinions of others to influence you. People often shy away from judgmental friends and acquaintances. Most people prefer relationships with those who are accepting and empathetic. Whether you are trying to enrich your relationships or hoping to overcome inborn prejudices, it can help to avoid passing judgment. By making an effort to understand others, focusing on shared humanity, and keeping watch of your judgmental quirks, you can improve your interactions with others.

You may even find you pass less judgment on yourself, which is just as damaging as the judgment you cast on others.

If you're serious about looking for the best in other people, not jumping to conclusions about their motives and inabilities, and giving them the benefit of the doubt that you ask for when you do something stupid, then you've got a supporter in me, brother.

1. ~~Impress~~
Impact

2. ~~Find followers~~
Make friends

3. Be ~~popular~~
yourself

Get Iconic

Reasons to take a guys' trip

- It's a time to reconnect instead of making excuses.

- It contains multitudes, from the super shallow and juvenile revisiting of your "good ole days" to the realities and depths of issues we face with wives, kids, and businesses.

- It allows you to open up about the questions and hypotheticals that take up space in our minds and cause feelings of inadequacy, uncertainty, fear, and imbalance.

- It provides, for me at least, instant feedback on why I don't drink and party like I used to (though some of my buddies show amazing skills in this category).

- It gives a glimpse into your friends' routines: who gets up early, who eats what, who calls home often, who packs eye cream (OK, I pack the eye cream . . .).

- It's a reminder that wealth comes in many forms: health, family, friendship, career, fitness, experiences, conversations, travel, camaraderie, and happiness.

- It lets you blow off steam without judgment of any kind and just laugh your ass off.

- It gives you insight on all sorts of adulting, including going through divorce, dealing with a kid's health issues, and being an empty nester. It's a reminder that everyone has their own problems and issues, and everyone has figured out their own way of handling them. You can't do it for them, and when everyone's struggles are put out there for all to hear, you end up wanting your own back.

- You can also just get fucked up. That's fine too.

Some takeaways from my last guys' trip:

- We all still check out all our "exes" and the "one-night stands" that truly stood out—what they're up to, who they married, how they look. It's hard to believe anyone actually chose to sleep with us back then, much less more than one time.

- Anything that happened in college and was funny then is still funny now. Just not to anyone who wasn't there.

- We established that there's a formula for the age of women we can still look at/date: "half your age plus seven."

- There's a fascination with the two foundational relationships in our lives: wives and careers, and are they "enough." Are we doing "enough," getting "enough," giving "enough," is it "enough"? But kids are never in question. I'm around some tremendous fathers.

- There's therapy . . . and a third of the guys are in it.

- We make decisions based on money, and that's not a bad thing. We have families, overhead, and lifestyles, and it takes time to figure out how to navigate them all. We've already put the years in, and starting over doesn't equate for some. For others, it's the opposite. Both are OK.

- Guys don't argue over who has the remote, where we're going to eat, or who wants to do what . . . We just do our thing. Twenty-four years or twenty-four hours . . . somehow it doesn't make that much of a difference. You can either hang or you can't. It's always been that way. Half the time we don't even say goodbye. It's perfect.

Sleepwalking

Don't do it, dude. I've seen too many guys get into their forties and fifties and sleepwalk through the biggies—birthdays, Christmas. They go through the motions on Mother's Day. They miss their kids' events, unless it's something they're interested in. You go to a son's basketball game but miss the daughter's dance recital? What kind of message do you think that sends? They justify it by saying they're working, but providing for your family doesn't give you an excuse to ignore the big moments or the mundane ones that result in connection with the people closest to you.

Sleepwalking takes many forms. They zone out in dinner conversations or when their woman is talking to them. They stay at the office an extra hour or bring an extra two hours of the office home with them. They stay at the gym an extra thirty minutes for an additional circuit, extra stretching, socializing, or the hot tub rather than coming home. They eat too much instead of leaving the dinner table to take part in other activities. They grab an extra beer, smoke a little too much pot. Hey, the buzz is enticing, but there's a time and a place.

What is so awful about sleepwalking is it's so condoned, by the individual and even by society. It's passive, a bomb waiting to explode with no ticking to give you any warning. The damage is real, but you can make enough excuses to keep it going for years without detection. People recognize the danger of a violent alcoholic, a verbally abusive tyrant in the house, a rude SOB. They tolerate a nice-enough guy who works hard and is tired a lot or self-medicating to a minor degree.

CHAPTER 7

It's Time to Break Up with Your Ego

Your ego takes you to some dark places.
It's not a healthy relationship.

I went to a small Division II school in Albany to play basketball. Unfortunately my discipline wasn't there in my twenties. Discipline became a thing at thirty-three. Which is funny because my dad was a football coach and my mom was a disciplinarian, and I did everything I could to push back. You spend most of your twenties trying to identify who you're going to become. Most of those things are predicated on the success of the people around you. If your buddies have success, you want to emulate that and you grade yourself against that. Most people—myself included—spend their twenties very insecure. In that insecurity I found myself saying, "Next year's my year." To get in shape, to make big money. But I wasn't very specific. As you get a little older and go through some of those trials and tribulations, you realize that the moment you stop grading yourself against somebody else, you give yourself the best opportunity to be successful.

I'm very transparent about my past. I had a horrible bout with alcohol, and I've been sober for six years. I'm a leader of 250 people, and I use that frequently in conversations. Sobriety teaches you discipline. I was a big partier. Went to rehab twice. It came to a head six years ago. I went into rehab with my father. The disappointment on his face taught me a lot, in that moment with him sitting next to me and the counselor said, "What do you for a living?"

I laughed and said, "I'm in the bar industry."

"You have to get out of that industry! You can't be in that industry if you have a problem with alcohol."

I said, "You're effin' crazy because this is my life."

She said, "Then you need to treat it as a business."

That comment and that discipline changed my life because it taught me a lot about priorities. I lose sight of that in moments, but overall my discipline has been laser focused. I can't believe the impact one sentence had on me. I needed that. Whether it's fitness or how we eat or how we act or interact with each other, those things all coincide with discipline. That's become a cornerstone of my life. So when I have moments of weakness, I'll punish myself for another week or two, but I'll also learn from it, and I'll learn how to make it better in a shorter amount of time. Instead of seven days, it will be five days. Then five days will be three days. And then one day it will be a fleeting moment. That's where I'm trying to get to. If I have an argument with someone, I'll spend time reflecting on how to curb that faster, because it's human nature.

We get emotional and protective about things. Ultimately, it's not about being right; it's about doing what's right.

— JOHN "JT" REED, owner/CEO of Bosscat Kitchen
& Libations and BCK Restaurant Group,
on *The Midlife Male* podcast, Episode #77

* * *

It takes discipline to break up with your ego. It also takes discipline not to punish yourself when you keep taking your ego back even after he treats you like a punching bag and puts you in positions you know you shouldn't be in. Keep at it though. You owe it to yourself and the people you surround yourself with to remind your ego that you are in charge.

I've had a long-standing toxic relationship with my ego.

Your ego tells you, "You deserve things."

You don't . . . You earn things.

Your ego tells you, "You're right and they are wrong."

They're not . . . You can simply agree to disagree.

Your ego tells you, "You can handle it yourself."

You can't. Nobody does anything alone.

Your ego tells you, "You need to be in control."

You're not. Control is relative.

Your ego tells you, "The only way you matter is if you're the center of attention."

It doesn't matter. Whether or not you're the winner, the "better" man, the richer or fitter person, nobody outside your ego really cares.

By breaking up with my ego, I have quietly found what I enjoy doing after thirty years of trial and error, failure and success.

It takes time. Lots of it. And tears, struggle, comparison, evaluation, victories, heartache, loss, disappointment, and joy. The good news is that over time you continually find what it is you don't like and what doesn't work. Ultimately, you start spending more time on what does.

When I took ego out of the equation, I learned that:

- All my hobbies don't need to become businesses.
- I don't need to be the boss.
- I don't need to win all the time.
- I don't need to compete every day.

I just need to do things that I enjoy with people I enjoy and focus on adding value.

Great work leads to more work.

Great people lead to more people.

By breaking up with my ego and my former beliefs that I needed to be in control, the entrepreneur, or the center of attention and that everything was actually about me, I've actually become more confident, valuable, and resourceful.

I'm able to provide a service, expertise, and experience that no one else in my industry has to offer. I'm able to once again enjoy activities, hobbies, and work that had become uncomfortable and caused strain.

There's no ego in that. It's letting go.

My ego used to have me constantly keeping score. I'd fixate on who didn't like me, didn't want to work with me, or didn't "get me." That's a draining and neg/ try and live.

Now I feed myself with words of encoura͓, belief that it's a big world out there; we're all different a͓. can make our own lives.

When you break up with our ego, you're left with what's real: rock-hard humility and confidence.

Whereas ego is artificial, this type of confidence can hold weight.

Ego is stolen; confidence is earned.

Ego blocks us from happiness; it stands in the way.

No wonder we find success empty.

No wonder we're exhausted.

No wonder it feels like we're on a treadmill.

No wonder we lose touch with the energy that once fueled us.

Get Naked

Leggo my ego

So how do you break up with your ego? Here are ten tips that I have found helpful:

1. Replace ego and resentment with empathy. This is a conscious and ongoing daily shift in mindset, and you won't do it perfectly right away. Just remember that you never know what someone else is going through. It's rarely about you.

2. Feed it. Do things that make you happy with people that make you happy. Avoid the things that don't.

3. Let go of bad habits. Replace tequila with coffee, TV with books, news with meditation and positive information.

4. Pump up your appearance. Exercise and take care of yourself. Step up your style. This isn't to impress others. It builds confidence for yourself. Physically craft the image you wish to project.

5. Walk the walk . . . and reduce your walks. This is the hardest one by far. However, by reducing the number of "walks" (I don't try to do everything anymore), I can focus more on being true and "walking the walk" in the things I do take on.

6. Practice forgiveness and letting go. As Mahatma Gandhi is quoted as saying, "The weak can never forgive. Forgiveness is the attribute of the strong."

7. Practice honesty and being open. Write it down if you have trouble saying it.

8. Surrender your need for control. You don't have to be the chairperson; you can simply volunteer. You don't need to own the gym; you can just go to the gym. You don't have to try and beat the system; you can navigate within the system.

9. Enjoy silent moments with yourself. Make the time for a stroll or bike ride. Sit still. Have coffee or a meal alone. Go for a drive. This isn't about escaping. It's about self-care *and* about making sure you are present when you are with others who deserve your full attention.

10. Practice gratitude. Write down three things each day that you are grateful for. This simple step to starting your day makes a huge positive impact.

Will you choose to live your life according to the demands and delusions of the ego or make the conscious intention to align yourself with kindness, appreciation, and security?

Choosing to always be conscious and to live according to our core values provides us with infinite possibilities and the peace, passion, and purpose that we all deserve as people.

Conversely, living unconsciously and according to the ego results in stress, unnecessary resistance, and much less desirable consequences. You deserve better, no matter what lines your ego is feeding you. Our ego is that voice within us that demands everything and pulls us along a path that is difficult and filled with obstacles. The ego robs us of the peace that we deserve and the opportunity to live our best possible lives. The ego interrupts this process with endless mind games.

Entrepreneurship is considered a young man's game, where energetic college students and twentysomethings incubate their new ideas into multimillion-dollar valuations. But more recent research fights this myth. A 2018 study in *American Economic Review: Insights* found that the average age at which a successful founder started a company is forty-five. If you think about it, this makes sense. Success in business requires learning more, knowing what to do with that learning—which often requires making mistakes for the lesson to resonate—and having the discipline to see it through. Sure, young, driven people are going to find success at an early age, but even they will find more success when they are older, I'd bet.

Success in life is no different, and relationships are at the heart of maximizing your time on this planet. It takes discipline to break up with your ego. When you do it, though, your connections with others will be that much better. There's no time like now to lean into that. Kick your ego to the curb and drive away stronger.

SH#T
YOUR
EGO
SAYS

Ten Things You Didn't Know About Me . . . and Now You Do

1. I'm very self-conscious about my left eye. It droops from an aneurysm/blood clot I had in my twenties. It's the only thing I see in pictures, which is why I wear sunglasses as often as possible and take most pictures not looking directly at the camera.

2. I pee sitting down quite often. I'm always on the go, always on my feet, and my legs are constantly sore, and this is one of the few times during the day I can sit down, relax, and take a moment.

3. I shave my head every Friday. I used to shave it on Sundays and then realized that I'm outside all weekend, training, with the kids, and doing whatever and that when I shaved my head on Sunday, the top of my head would be white and my face would be tan.

4. I cry almost daily. Could be a song, something my boys do, a movie, or a commercial. I love the sad, sappy, inspirational shit.

5. I like violent activities. Boxing, combat, shooting, throwing around heavy shit. Love it all and the idea of using strength and force to protect people.

6. I am extremely loyal and trusting. However, trust but verify. If I verify you can't be trusted, we're done.

7. I don't like to read. I'm always getting books and looking at magazines but rarely finish anything.

8. I love writing but I have trouble sitting down to "write," so I talk instead. I use voice notes or Otter and then transcribe, so I constantly look like I'm talking to myself. I've written 146 newsletters, two guides, and a forthcoming book this way.

9. I want to move to the beach, someplace like Cabo or Costa Rica, live off a fixed income, wake up, drink coffee with Kate, watch the sunrise, surf, write, podcast, coach a few clients, work out, eat great foods, watch the sunset with Kate, and repeat. Have the boys and their friends visit often.

10. I battle stress, anxiety, body image, imposter syndrome, and social disorder daily. I am only comfortable in a few places around a few people. If you think all the things I do come easy or naturally to me, they do not.

CHAPTER 8

I Miss Every Monday

Give your body and mind a chance
to take a day off.

When my wife met me, I was a bartender. She didn't know life was going to go the direction it went. Owning a restaurant was a dream of mine, and I would feed her all the dreams that I had as I was building this career. Because I was able to create this business and generate some revenue for our family, about three years into operating The Meatball Shop, I'd worked to the bone. I'd worked so much that I never saw her. She was very busy in her modeling career, but I didn't take a day off for eighteen months straight when I opened up the restaurant for the first business. She looked at me and said, "Mike, I love you to death and I want to build a family with you, but it can't be this way. It just can't. It's not fair to you, and it's not fair to me. I need more of you."

I knew in my heart of hearts that she was absolutely right, and I also knew that I wanted to build a family with this wonderful woman, and I would never find somebody quite like her ever again. She just makes me so happy. She's my best friend. I said, "We've got to get out of New York on weekends, because if I'm in New York, it's going to be very hard for me not to physically be in the workplace." We rented a house with a couple of friends just to see if it was possible for me to do it. We ended up going up at least twice a month to the Catskills. After a year of that, we decided to look to buy a place. I had sold a little equity in The Meatball Shop, so I had some capital. We looked for about six months until we found this unbelievable property. We did it, and we're up here two or three times a month on the weekends. It's a line that I've drawn thick in the sand where I've told my partner, I work my ass off, and I'm not going to subject my family to not seeing me and me not seeing them. I want to be part of their upbringing. I don't work on the weekends, period.

Mentally and physically, it's hard to be present upstate with them. The weekend is the busiest time in the restaurant business. I still struggle with it. Just because I remove myself from the concrete jungle of New York City doesn't mean my head isn't focused on business and the abundance of emails that are still coming in all day Saturday and Sunday. I have to really practice separation from it. There are times when my wife will be like, "You are so not here, at all." It's hard for me not to get frustrated and say, "Do you know what it's like to get a hundred emails on a Saturday?" It's an ongoing practice. I do believe we'll come to a point, hopefully sooner rather than later, where this nonstop constant accessibility, unrealistic response times from business that this has to stop.

I try my best to leave it in the city when I head upstate, and I would say I do pretty well. I do give myself a couple hours on Sunday morning to sift through and get through as many emails as I can before Monday morning comes around. But it's an ongoing battle.

— **MICHAEL CHERNOW,** founder of Seamore's restaurants and cofounder of The Meatball Shop, on *The Midlife Male* podcast, Episode #38

* * *

When you scroll through social media, do you get bombarded with bullshit Carpe Monday Diem motivational quotes?

- "Never miss a Monday."
- "Monday sets the tone for the week. Crush it."
- "Rule #1 to working out: never skip Monday!"
- "Mondays belong to the go-getters."

What's Latin for "Slow the fuck down, Caesar?"

I'm not singing "I Don't Like Mondays" each week by any means. (Happens to be a great song though.) But if you need that much motivation to get you up on a Monday, maybe you've got bigger problems.

Whether it's drawing a thick line in the sand on no-work weekends or choosing a day off from working out or making a commitment to not skimp on sleep, you have to give yourself breaks and time to recover. To win the day ahead, you've got to win the night before, which means getting plenty of sleep. You make the schedule that works for you, but plugging in consistent downtime is nonnegotiable.

I actually love Mondays (sorry, Bob Geldof). I've flipped "Never miss a Monday" to "I miss every Monday."

I tend to go pretty hard, and as hard as I like to go, it's also important to slow down. Part of maximizing middle age is knowing when to go hard and when you need to recover.

I'll redline it Tuesday through Friday with work and projects. On the weekends, I'm all about life experiences, spending time with my family, and being active. That takes a lot of energy and puts a lot of strain on my body and mind, so Mondays are typically my slowdown day.

When Monday comes around, I like to be mindful, express gratitude, refocus, restore, rejuvenate, revisit my goals, and take small, positive action steps. In that way, I ease into the new week.

Here are some typical Monday tasks and activities for me:

- I'll sleep in a little. For me, that's 6:00 or 6:30 a.m.
- Take my dogs to the park and then drop them off to get a bath.
- Get my car washed. A clean truck after a weekend of off-road activities just makes me feel good.
- Go over my goals for the quarter and the rest of the year and update them.
- Set up a few calls to make sure projects are on schedule and aligned.
- Touch base with some clients.
- Make a couple of outreach calls.
- Take a long sauna.
- Spend a few minutes in the cold plunge.

- Take a walk or ride my bike.
- Meditate for a few minutes.
- Check in with a good friend or two.
- Read a couple articles on places I want to go, things I want to see, and topics I want to explore.
- Have dinner with the family.
- Get to bed early.

I believe in working hard and playing harder, but I'm not talking about the recovering-from-your-hangover type of playing harder from in your twenties. I'm talking about recovering from good, hard, wholesome work that's physically, spiritually, and mentally taxing—the fun stuff that fills your tank and feels great but can also drain it because it's exhausting.

When you put so much into everything, it takes so much out of you as well. You've got to take the time to charge back up again.

How to Have a Nice Day

We all get busy and overwhelmed. So much so that we often forget to just simply have a nice day.

More often than not, that's enough.

Enough to change our mood, put things back in perspective, breathe, practice gratitude, and be thankful and appreciative for what we do have in our lives rather than what we do not.

Here are some basic things I do to have a nice day:

a good night's sleep

ke up without an alarm clock

ss my wife

- Have breakfast as a family
- See the kids off to school
- Exercise
- Put in a good day's work
- Walk my dogs
- Take a bath
- Have a clean, simple dinner
- Call, text, or write a nice note to a couple of friends
- Get into bed early with a good book or movie

It doesn't need to be more complicated than that. Mondays don't require motivation. They require consistency, discipline, and resolve.

A subtle shift in mindset toward valuing what is present and right in front of you and maximizing the life you're living, not the one you're chasing.

Keep it simple.

Teach Gratitude

Aaron Hinde, cofounder and president of LIFEAID beverage company, suggests asking your kids each day three things that they're grateful for and also sharing three things that you are grateful for. I did it with my boys when they were younger. It's great for when they're a captive audience, such as in the car on the way to practice or school or in line somewhere.

The Second F
FITNESS

- [ ] Do you like the way you look?
- [ ] Are you comfortable with your sex life?
- [ ] Do you wake up tired?
- [ ] Where do you do your best thinking?
- [ ] What do you think about when you're sitting on the toilet?
- [ ] What is your favorite type of exercise?
- [ ] Do you look at yourself in the mirror?
- [ ] Do you meditate?
- [ ] What makes you feel inspired?
- [ ] Do you still play and stay active?

CHAPTER 9

The Difference between Resolution and Resolve

Take action to get out of a rut.

I remember the day I made the decision to lose my weight as clear as if it were yesterday. I'd gone to a two-year school. I'd gone to the University of Oklahoma. Found out Disney was hiring so I dropped out of school. Went to Disney, worked there for a couple years. I thought I really needed to go finish school, auditioned, and got a theater scholarship at Rollins College, and dropped out of school again. I had a scholarship that paid for classes, but I had no money as far as living expenses. That last semester at Rollins, my apartment literally was a mattress on the floor, no box springs, a TV, and I was living off a box of Minute Rice. And I wish I could tell you that I was exaggerating this and writing this script. My mom and dad knew I had three maxed-out credit cards, because those bills and overdue notices were coming back to the house. My mom said, "I really think you should come home." It was like a punch in my gut, because I knew she was right. So I gave up on that dream and moved back home. Three-time college dropout, one hundred pounds overweight, not pursuing any acting, tending bar in north Dallas.

One morning I was upstairs. I had taken a shower, and usually when you're a hundred pounds overweight. you don't hover in front of the mirror a whole lot when you come out of the shower. For whatever reason that day, I did. I didn't respect the person in the mirror. Like it was yesterday, I could hear these audible voices saying, "Who is going to love this? If you don't do something, this is it, Jimmy." I was twenty-two at the time. "If you don't do something, you're going to be alone and living with your parents. You're going to be that guy."

My life didn't change overnight that day. It wasn't like I was super motivated and found the answer to all my life problems, but there was a shift. When I work with clients, there's always that enough-is-enough moment: When did the pain get so bad that it was worse to stay where you were than to move?

— **JIMMY HAYS NELSON,** former actor, life coach, and
Beachbody partner, on *The Midlife Male* podcast,
Episode #85

* * *

I asked you to check yourself out in the mirror at the start of this book. Jimmy did that years ago and scared the shit out of himself. He embodies the reflection and transformation that all of us are capable of. Good, bad, or ugly, he had the same strengths, weaknesses, resources, and support network available to him before he stepped into the shower that day as he did when he stepped out. To assert that you are going to make a change and to actually do it are two radically different things.

I'm tired of hearing about resolutions. And I'm not just talking about New Year's! What we should really be focused on is resolve. There's a subtle yet important difference between a resolution and resolve.

A resolution is defined as a decision to do or not do something.

Resolve is defined as a firm determination to do something.

Read that again.

Now let it sink in.

Which one are you?

How do you want to be perceived?

The wishy-washy, noncommitted resolution guy, or the clearly focused, results-oriented resolve man?

It's not too late.

In fact, it's never too late.

If you're the former, I challenge you to go back and make the change from "Here are my resolutions" to "I resolve to do the following."

That's big. That's impactful.

Anyone can make a resolution. Very few have resolve.

If you've made a resolution, it's too easy to blame circumstances and others if your goal goes sideways. If you resolve to do something, it means you're taking responsibility and not letting obstacles get in the way of the change *you* have committed to making.

We've all *tried* to make changes, only to find someone else to point the finger at when we failed.

That reality exposes the lack of integrity in a resolution.

Resolve doesn't try; resolve just does. The integrity—and the success—is in the doing.

Resolve doesn't mean you won't have setbacks that require creative solutions.

Resolve just means you will keep moving because you've already chosen the result and moving is required to get you there.

Here are some ways to turn your resolutions into resolve.

Must be quantifiable. "Exercise more" and "make more money" are general statements and won't help you get anywhere. Get specific. Ten minutes of meditation per day. Three HIIT workouts per week and walk for one hour two days per week. Read for thirty minutes per day. Limit social media to one hour per day. Increase my income by 20 percent by selling cyber insurance to existing clients who currently don't carry it. You get the point.

Write it *all* down. We have a running joke (but it's very serious) in our house that if it's not on the calendar, it doesn't exist. That's everything: workouts, meditation, family dinner, new business calls, writing this newsletter ... it's all on the calendar, and it all has *time* clearly allocated to it and reminders set. Deadlines and timelines establish accountability and discipline.

Be results driven. Busy sucks. Productivity rules. Focus on the results you want, and then put in the minimum effective dose to achieve your goal. Your goal should inspire and motivate you each day, not scare you into not wanting to get out of bed. Take your goals and break them down into measurable and manageable pieces. How do you eat an elephant? One bite at a time!

Reward yourself. It's important to taste victory. To enjoy the journey and the process as much as the result. Rather than wait until the end of the year or accomplishment of your "big" goal" to celebrate, reward yourself when you hit certain milestones. When I land a client of X new revenue, I book a trip to someplace new. Point is, don't wait. This year, toss the useless resolutions and commit to having the resolve to achieve your goals.

Motivational speaker Les Brown tells the story of an old man sitting next to a dog that is yelping in pain. A boy walks by.

"What's wrong with the dog?" the boy asks.

"He's sitting on a nail," replies the old man.

"Well, why doesn't he move?"

"Oh," the old man says, "he doesn't hurt enough to move. He just hurts enough to moan and groan about it."

How bad are you hurting?

When is the fear of moving finally not greater than the fear of standing still?

I would add that the dog must be a male, because he refuses to ask for help from the old man (see chapter 7 on how to put your ego in the basement and be willing to seek support when you don't know the answer).

Get Moving

Choose resolve over resolution

Choosing resolve over resolution is relevant to all the Fs in this book. Don't miss opportunities to resolve to change what you need to do differently to live a better life and be a positive influence on those closest to you:

- Resolve to be intentional about what you put into and onto your body.

- Resolve to make the financial decisions that will give you liberty and options.

- Resolve to repair or extract yourself from the relationships that are creating stress and negativity in you and others.

- Resolve to be conscious and caring about where you stick your dick.

- Resolve to make fun and experiences at least as important as work and things.

- Resolve to see the value of integrity and legacy and be smart about how to leave both intact when you no longer have the choice between being a noun or a verb—when you trade in one adjective (alive) for another (dead).

Genetic Predisposition

Often I get asked about my training and nutrition, but my response is applicable to all aspects of life:

There's no one size fits all. There is no perfect.

What I do may or may not work for you.

You may or may not see similar results.

Focus on being the best that you are genetically predisposed to be. What I mean by that is that all of us will respond differently to stimuli. I may be genetically blessed with better-responding abs, but at the same time I'm bald and apparently am predisposed to torn retinas.

We all want what we don't have or can't have, but rather than look at others and try to chase or replicate their goals, patterns, habits, or results, focus on being the best version of yourself.

Aggregate knowledge from experts and continue to learn, and then apply *only* what applies and works for you.

We're all unique individuals.

Focus on maximizing your genetic predisposition and your own version of total life wellness.

CHAPTER 10

Handle Stress Like a (Vulnerable) Man

Be open enough to accept ways to deal with difficult times.

For women, when we really tap into the nervous system and get things to finally calm down—especially when you have pain, things are hot, things are a little bit more on the surface, a little bit more touchy because it's like, Why do I have this pain? I shouldn't have this pain. It needs to go away. I don't have time for it. A lot of things happen around pain and injury and the body, especially emotionally and how we handle it in our nervous system, that we don't even realize. I've had a lot of women who start crying. A lot of times they don't know why they're crying. They don't understand what's happening, but their body is finally releasing. When we're really tapping into this different level of the nervous system, I find

I get there quicker with women. Some men, it takes a lot more verbal communication. It's more analytical, like, Let me understand what is happening, because I'm not just going to cry for you. So we have to talk through things more. That's what I find more with men. That's not bad. I've had a lot of success with men, tapping them back into the nervous system. It just takes a little longer, and it takes different avenues to get there. Coming from a woman standing in front of you, it's hard to say I'm going to fully let go or fully tell you everything that I'm feeling. Maybe if I was a male therapist, I'd create a different space.

A man wants to feel like he can do it for himself. I have a lot of men in my programs and a lot of males learning with me. The success where that's coming from is that they see what can be beneficial, maybe not in person, but I have these tools online. I see men having success online and feeling that empowerment of "I did it! I was able to make this change," which is ultimately my whole goal with every human, male or female. I want them to feel empowered that they took tools with their body and created change. If that's the avenue that people can get there from, I'm all for it.

I started working in a physical therapy clinic, and I got so fascinated watching a therapist feel movement in their hands or watch movement from someone who is just walking. I wondered, What are they watching? I loved being in the clinic being able to see clients. It's not seeing them in a doctor's office and wondering if the thing you're telling them to do is actually going to be done. You're actually walking the journey with someone. I loved that aspect. It feels genuine to me. I wanted to walk journeys with people. I didn't care how many loans. I didn't care what I needed to do. I was going to be a physical therapist.

— **DR. JEN ESQUER,** creator of the Mobility Method and cohost of *The Optimal Body Podcast*, on *The Midlife Male* podcast, Episode #120

* * *

Whether their stress is physical or emotional, men have a tendency to not allow themselves to get vulnerable. We don't want to acknowledge how we feel or to risk looking awkward. Yeah, that's a blanket statement, and I recognize some guys are far more willing to "go there" than I used to be.

But there's also science to back up the statement. When it comes to the fight-or-flight syndrome that has kick-started our adrenal system in stressful situations since the dawn of time, three hormones are called to action: cortisol, epinephrine, and oxytocin. Men release less oxytocin than women do, and since oxytocin relaxes the emotions, it tends to make women more likely to nurture and reach out.

Men are more likely to compartmentalize and repress the emotions determining whether they will fight or run away. Men more often turn to competition or threats as an opportunity to show they can win, thus "solving the problem" in a way that never requires acknowledgment of their feelings.

Writing in the past tense

Past or present tense. Which are you? This isn't a grammar lesson now.

I know there's all this talk about being present, how you need to be present, present, present, present. Nope. Get away from that. Get past it.

Now, when it comes to anxiety, I do my best to operate in the past tense. For a lot of my life, I operated in the present tense. That is . . . I was always tense. You can't do anything well when you're tense.

If you're anything like me and you're constantly feeling tension, why would you want to hang out in the present tense? That's where the tension is. It's present! Naturally you'd want to get past the tension in order to move forward.

See what I'm saying? You want to get "past tense," right?

That's where I hang out now. It feels better.

And it requires vulnerability—sharing with others who can be helpful and supportive, and being honest with yourself about the difficulties you face.

One of the reasons I started writing in the first place was because I was always tense. Things were getting to me, and I was having trouble getting past them. Writing was and still is a way for me to work through tension I'm feeling. I can sit down and journal about the experience or just mouth off into the voice memos on my iPhone while in my car—say anything I need to say and get it out of my system.

And just like invoking the twenty-four-hour rule on an email (write it, give it twenty-four hours, the read it again before send it), I didn't have to do anything with it (or I could turn it into a newsletter that thousands now read every Sunday). I could vent, put it down on paper, read it back the next day, think about whether I was completely irrational, learn from it, and often laugh at it.

It didn't matter, because I had absolutely no control over the other individual or situations that were making me tense in the first place. What I know now is that I only have control over myself. I was allowing these things to make me physically and mentally tense. If I didn't find a way to listen, not react, and subsequently alleviate the tension, I was destined to have a constant pain in my neck and scoff on my brow for the rest of my life.

How do you deal with stress?

Here's a list of things that seem to help me get in the past tense. Yes, you can spend a lot of time working to *relieve* tension, but trust me, the better option is spending less time around things that cause it.

Perhaps you've got others to add to the list. Whatever works for you, good on you for taking the energy and possibly the trial and error to find it. Treasure that gift, and pass it on to other guys who are struggling to get there.

- Writing
- Audio notes
- Exercise (Be careful here, too much HIIT can actually cause more tension)
- Ice baths
- Warm Epsom salt baths
- Saunas
- Walks
- Meditation
- Box breathing

- Pets
- Saying *no*
- Being outside
- Yoga
- CBD oil
- Melatonin
- Music, playing or listening to it
- PMR: Progressive Muscle Relaxation. Research shows that relaxing your body physically can also release psychological tension and stress, minimizing your stress reactivity and decreasing your experience of chronic stress. There are other effective ways to minimize psychological and emotional stress, but PMR can offer you one more tool to manage stress, which can help you to build your resilience overall.

I'm constantly experimenting with techniques that help me reduce stress. There's not one solution that works for everyone or even one solution that works for each of us. Add to the tools in your stress toolbox the way you add to the toolbox in your garage.

Let the physical enhance the mental

For years, if I had to choose between a hard workout or a mobility workout, you know which one I would choose, right?

You'd better believe I wanted to get the adrenaline pumping and do what I thought was going to make me feel like I was active. Even better, it was an opportunity to let out aggression when I felt like I needed that.

As you see in my list above, there is a mix of active, relaxing, and cognitive activities. As I've gotten older and I build out my weekly fitness schedule (I calendar everything!), far more often I'll emphasize longevity and lean into exercises that generate flow, body awareness, balance, endurance, strength, and mobility while leaving space for fun and play—functional activities that help me stand, sit, pick up and put things down, and move better in all directions. I train to be able to perform the things I need to do in real life at a high level.

At the same time, I wonder if my choices are also a recognition that I need more space in my life for reflection rather than action. I sometimes ponder how people manage stress, the effects that stress has on us, and why some people seem better equipped to handle stress than others.

A lot of my stress comes from expectations, specifically my unrealistic expectations of others. I expect people, colleagues, clients, friends, and family to act, react, or behave a certain way. When they don't, it creates tension, as I have a difficult time understanding, accepting, and taking a pragmatic, impersonal, and unemotional approach to how I respond to and handle these types of situations.

It so happens that when I expect everyone in my orbit to do things my way, results don't always go as planned. Shocking, I know.

Alternatively, I intentionally put myself in stressful physical situations every day. In this manner, my body and mind respond very well to processing stressful physical situations: in the water, on a mountain, in the weight room, in a ring. I'm able to control my breathing, heart rate, temperament, and demeanor much better. I can identify and work through these types of stressful situations much more clearly and naturally.

I'm in charge of the situation, and I don't need validation or a response of any kind to get to a better place. That's better for me, and it's better for those around me. Sometimes, you need to confront others to get at the root of a stressful situation, but awareness that in most situations it is folly to control others will give you far more control in putting you in your best space. For me, the physical stress helps me to reduce the mental stress.

Be uncomfortable for the right reasons

You've heard about the importance of getting out of your comfort zone, and that's true. But be aware of why you're doing it. Getting uncomfortable keeps you sharp, curious, evolving mentally and physically. When you think you *have* to do something and justify it with, "Well, getting out of my comfort zone is a good thing, right?" ... then you've got a problem.

Over the years, I've stressed myself out by putting myself in places and situations where I was always pushed to perform better. I told myself it built character if I forced myself to be in uncomfortable situations, around uncomfortable people, clients, meetings, business ventures, partnerships, and teams. I even succumbed to a schedule that was uncomfortable.

All it did was make me miserable.

Much of this came down to fear of not conforming, of missing out, of not doing things the way everybody else does them, or that's just life—that's the way we do it here or the way it should be done.

Be uncomfortable for the right reasons. These were not the right reasons.

I spent so much time and energy trying to fix my weaknesses and failures and be something I'm not rather than focusing and putting all my energy and time into capitalizing on the strengths I do have and thriving in places and situations where I feel comfortable.

I'm asking different and better qualifying questions up front now. I'm managing expectations a lot differently. I'm seeking out certain types of people in certain types of industries who want to work a certain type of way.

Is avoidance always the best way to manage stress? No, not necessarily.

Are there still uncomfortable situations that I find myself in? Absolutely.

There is a lot that I cannot control, that I have to get over and get past that causes stress, inhibits growth, limits productivity, and has an adverse effect on my physical and mental health.

But I'm taking the steps necessary to reduce the frequency and severity of the flare-ups. That's what being a vulnerable man is all about.

We're Not in Competition

- [ ] I can be happy for you and focused on my own goals.

- [ ] When you need help and someone helps you, say "thank you."

- [ ] When someone needs help and you help them, that's the "thank you."

- [ ] Try allowing rather than forcing.

That's how you win.

CHAPTER 11

Picture This: Be a Better Version of You

Put yourself out there to improve
and inspire yourself.

I'm that fitness and sports nerd. I started going to gyms when I was eight years old. My father was in the Army, but he was stationed at an air force base at one point. I remember Spangdahlem, Germany. I'm in there watching these airmen lift all these weights, and I got intrigued by it. From there, you go to the military installations' gyms. They had everything. Basketball. Racquetball. Swimming pools, so you had diving. There were all these activities, and I started playing all of them. I have competed in more organized events—and I'm not just talking about going down with your buddies on Saturday to play some volleyball or whatever; I'm talking leagues. When I look at exercise and fitness, up until a couple months ago,

I have never worked out for aesthetic reasons. I have always worked out to do something to be better at some sporting activity. I had always looked at the aesthetic portion of it as a by-product of an amazing workout program. I never stopped working out, because I never stopped playing. I was always playing something.

Now at my age, I cannot compete against most men who are my age. It's a joke. I have to compete against guys who are half my age, because most men who are my age don't do all these things. I'll get out there and play basketball and I'm playing against these twenty-four-, twenty-five-year-olds, and I'm still getting up above the rim. I remember going to 24 Hour Fitness a few years back. I'm jumping around getting rebounds and one of these guys is like, "Aw, man, wait till you get my age. You're gonna get those bad knees. You're not gonna be jumping around like that anymore." I was like, "OK, how old are you?" He was like, "Man, I'm thirty-nine years old." I was like, "All right." I didn't tell him I was forty-seven at the time. I've never stopped doing those things, because I love to play. I love to compete.

— **MILO BRYANT,** founder and head coach at the Coalition for Launching Active Youth, on *The Midlife Male* podcast, Episode #121

* * *

You don't stop playing because you get old; you get old because you stop playing. That saying has always stuck with me because it's my mindset toward working out and toward living. The aesthetics are just a bonus. The real mental and physical fulfillment is in training to be good at life!

Yeah, I post a bunch of pictures on social media with my shirt off and working out. Guilty as charged.

I'm sure there are guys out there who think I'm just trying to show off or that I'm an egotistical douchebag (that's certainly possible, but I've been working hard to get past all that).

Posting pictures and engaging with other executive athletes and like-minded guys who are still pushing their physical limits has a very specific purpose: it holds me accountable publicly and privately. Pictures serve as a form of motivation, inspiration, and self-expression.

And if it inspires even just one person to take better care of themselves, then it's worth it.

I'm proud of and still striving to be the best version of myself that I can be. Moving well, having energy, being able to perform at a high level, and being healthy feels awesome.

The aesthetics are a bonus.

The power of a picture

I got a call from a client and friend. He told me that he was preparing for his son's bar mitzvah and went to look at some pictures from his daughter's bat mitzvah a few years earlier. He couldn't believe what he looked like then and how much he had let himself go. It was a tipping point for him. Sometimes that's all it takes: a picture, seen at the right time and moment when you're ready to take a good hard look at yourself.

He made a commitment to change his lifestyle, reclaim his health, and become a better version of himself for this upcoming special occasion. Thirty pounds lighter, he's a new man—energized, confident, motivated. That type of transformation translates into all aspects of life too. Nobody can make you do it. You just have to want it.

If you're not in the condition you want to be in, get out your camera and take a picture of yourself. You don't have to post it on social media. Just stick it on your mirror or someplace where you can see it. Then get to work. Keep taking pictures of yourself, and document your progress. Think you'll want to go back to the "old you" once "new you" has arrived?

Snapshot everything

Now, apply the same principle to other areas of your life. Write down your life goals, and take a photo of them. Take a picture of your bank statement, credit card bill, the house you want to live in, the car you want to drive, the college your kids want to go to, places you want to visit, you name it.

Then apply consistency, discipline, execution, and a positive attitude to becoming a better husband, father, provider, person.

Chances are you're already doing this successfully in some aspect of your life. Now do it in all of them. We all have room for improvement. The best simply get up, show up, and outwork the rest.

Enlist others' support

My father passed away at forty-seven. Long before I ever reached that age, not a day went by that I didn't think about how he never got to experience the second act of his life. I have no intention of slowing down or to stop playing and competing anytime soon. The sweat, nutrition, sleep, sacrifice, recovery, time, and money are all worth it to me.

You either get the lifestyle or you don't. For us like-minded guys, it's in our DNA. If you don't, it's not too late. Age is just a number. It doesn't matter what stage in life you're at right now. Midlife doesn't mean crisis. It should be the time to live our best and brightest lives. You can start anytime, but *you* have to take the first step.

My experience is that there are plenty of helpful people at the gym or any physical activity who want to inspire and motivate others to discover the many benefits of their sweat of choice. And yet, many men whose egos are as big as their waistline don't take advantage of the opportunities that are all around us—men who would never run their businesses as poorly as they run their lives.

How many times over the past decade have I tried to encourage a friend or client to join me at the gym? "Oh," they say, "I need to get in shape before I work out with you."

I hear this all the time, and it frustrates the shit out of me. Dude, that's the point: to *get* in shape.

That's the equivalent of me saying, "I can't have a conversation with you because you're smarter than me."

Sounds ridiculous, right?

You don't get in shape to work out. You work out to get in shape.

I've pulled a few sleds and done a few pull-ups and barbell rows in my day. Of course I'm going to do these exercises a ton better than you. Unless you've done a movement or a rep three thousand times, you aren't allowed to get upset with yourself when you don't do it just right. I guarantee I won't laugh at you; I'll give you tips so you can get better at it.

You know who is open to tips? Women. They aren't threatened by a workout partner who can help them, and they're not afraid of looking stupid. Women are willing to try anything that works for whatever their goal is.

Look, I get it. In areas where you are confident, you are willing to take a chance and look silly. We feel like we can push ourselves and eventually figure it out after a few tries. But in other areas, we put limits on ourselves. We quit if we struggle on our first try.

Start saying yes to being the best version of yourself.

Stop putting pressure on the outcome and instead embrace the process.

And there's always room for another guy in that club. Photo ID included.

Get Naked

If you've got it, flaunt it. So get it.
I wanted so badly to hit the snooze button this morning.

That's the easy choice. The instant gratification decision. The short-term pacification of what can become a permanent problem. When we have a particularly challenging week, mentally, physically, or emotionally, that's when we need to stick to our routine the most.

Lean on it for support and to release the past.

> We are what we consistently do. Create your morning routine. The rest of your day will follow suit. Complacency is the enemy. Find what works for you. Experiment. Try new things. When you find what works, make it a habit. Make it a lifestyle—your lifestyle. You only get one life. Make the most of it.

This Is What Authentic Looks Like

I'm not a tough guy. Some of my imagery doesn't match the man I am.

Yes, I train (a lot). I'm into violent contact activities, heavy physical exertion, and intense personal challenges that some may view as extreme. But I'm actually soft.

This stuff is just fun for me. It brings me joy and takes me outside of my comfort zone. It helps me to cope and has supported me through stress, anxiety, depression, loss, addiction, insecurity, hopelessness, anger, frustration.

I don't like confrontation. I'm incredibly shy. I'm uncomfortable and sweat profusely in most public situations (which is why working out is great, because nobody can tell the difference between nervous sweat and training sweat). Rarely do I think I look good or perform well at anything.

I take way too many things personally (still). If I succeed at three things, I'll fixate on the fourth thing I failed at. I don't mind being bald, but I really don't want to be fat and bald. I'd stay in and hang out with my family and dogs all day, every day if I could.

When I go places, I always feel like people are looking at me and I don't fit in. I talk way too much in situations as I'm hoping time will just run out and I can leave. By the end of every week, I'm exhausted because everything seems to take so much out of me and everything is really, really hard.

I genuinely do not know how anyone accomplishes anything, as I constantly feel like I either have too much time or not enough time. I suffer from severe paralysis by analysis.

I carry guilt, resentment, and humility everywhere, and yet I can be perceived as arrogant and standoffish. I'd like a few more good friends, but I don't know if I'm selfless enough to be a really good friend in return.

I cry weekly. I'll read an article, see a picture, get off a call, someone will ask me something about my kids . . . anything might bring tears. I'm an emotional train wreck.

So, if you're reading this book, checking out my Instagram, or listening to the podcast, I'm grateful. Mostly, though, I want you to know that I'm working through life just like you are. I don't have it all figured out. I'm learning, listening, being curious, and just doing the best I can.

CHAPTER 12
Where Do You Find Your Drive?

Work hard *and* give your body a break.

Looking back, when I was sixteen, seventeen, eighteen, nineteen years old, I didn't like someone telling me what to do. If someone said, "Hey, man, can you pick up that piece of paper and hand it to me," I didn't like it. That was immaturity, of course. I look back at some things and I realize I had a bad attitude too. Getting into the fitness side, that was something I actually wanted to do. I liked working out, and I wanted to get more involved.

I applied to a supplement company, and I applied to be a trainer at a gym. Boom, I got hired on as a trainer at 24 Hour Fitness. That's when my career started taking off, because I fell in love with helping people and encouraging people and seeing people changing their body. Nothing against the big franchise gyms, but it's always about hitting a number. To me, it was more about wanting to help people. I don't want to just take their money and say, "OK, at least I hit my number

. . . but did I change anybody? Did I have any cool transforma-
tions? Do I have any stories to tell at the end of this month?"

That's when I went independent. I said I wasn't going to
do this anymore because I felt like I was just trying to hit a number. It's just a number. What's in your bank account? What the
scale says. What your age is. They're all just numbers.

Encouraging and helping people started with myself,
competing in bodybuilding. That's how the whole Drive thing
started, really. It was about me competing against myself and
figuring out how am I going to push myself to go farther. So
I tattooed it on me. It was something to look down at between
my reps and sets to tell myself I've got to keep pushing. I've
gotta keep that drive; I've gotta keep going in life. I can't stop.

I tell myself I'm only going to do ten reps, so I'm just going to stop at ten because I easily got ten?! No. Force me to
get those extra reps in life. Don't just get those extra reps in
the gym, get those extra reps in life too. Go the extra mile. If
your boss tells you, "Hey, man, I just need you to clean this
room," clean his office too. Who cares, do that extra thing in
life, and stop doing the mediocre and just saying I'm going to
stop right here at ten reps because my trainer told me to do
three sets of ten. Dude, he's just setting a number for you. If
you can go past that, go past it. That's what I encourage to all
my legends—that's what I call my clients—just because I write
out a workout for you and tell you to do this, you can switch
it up or add more reps to it. If you feel like you can do more,
do more. If you can go past it, go beyond it.

— **CHAD LEMONS,** founder of The Drive Clothing
company and The Drive Diet Program, on *The
Midlife Male* podcast, Episode #33

* * *

You won't find many people with more energy than Chad. The Lone Wolf is an inspiring entrepreneur, bodybuilder, and social media influencer in all the best of ways. His motivation is literally written all over his body, and his full-throttle mantra is literally the name of his businesses: Drive.

He's the Lone Wolf, yet he loves working with people. He didn't like being told what to do as a kid (who does?), but now he has built up the credibility to do just that to others who believe in him. He channeled his rebellion into something positive and flipped the script. Chad nudges his legends to reach farther and seek their limits, but he's not telling them to hurt themselves in the process. If you can do more reps, do them. If you can't . . . do what you can today, and live to fight tomorrow.

Even Special Forces take a break

I've said many times you've got to give your body a chance to rest and recover. That's true at any age and especially at midlife. Push yourself and go hard when you work and play, then cherish your down time. That's how you let your story continue, long and healthy.

There's a military workout program called SOFLETE that I follow. Essentially, the data was showing that Special Forces soldiers were overtraining to the point where they could not perform their duties effectively in the field and were getting injured frequently.

What's the point of training if you can't actually perform when called upon? What's the point of looking the part if you can't act the part? Imagine Tom Brady doing a burner workout and endless miles of rucking with an eighty-pound pack every day leading up to the Super Bowl. How would he play? Not great, right? But that's essentially what many other military fitness companies were asking from their users.

Now, we're not Special Forces guys and we're not playing in the Super Bowl, but you get the point. This principle can and should be applied to our everyday lives as Midlife Males. What's the point of being so overconditioned that I can't take a bike ride with my son? (If you're so underconditioned that you can't do it, we need to have a different conversation altogether.)

A hard night's day

Sometimes I push too hard because I forget I'm not twenty years old with no responsibilities other than getting to an econ class that starts at 11:00 a.m. We had friends over last night. That doesn't happen too often and we had a great time, but, man, does it throw my shit off balance.

Here's why. Dinner goes longer. Instead of quitting after dinner, it turns into coming back to our place, which turns into having another drink, which turns into 11:00 p.m. (not exactly late, but for me it is), which turns into texting my workout partner that I now can't make a 9:00 a.m. track workout, which turns into a shitty night's sleep because I don't usually drink and it gets me off my routine.

So, I wake up late, with a headache, not wanting to sit at the computer and write . . . Fuck! Now I'm thrown off my game mentally and physically. The kids are awake . . . it's 7:55 instead of 5:55 . . . Chances of morning sex . . . zero.

But . . .

I need this every once in a while. It's a little reminder that I create my own story. I remember why I prefer day over night and being sober instead of drinking . . . why I like waking up with energy and clarity as opposed to reaching for the Advil and a blanket.

What would Carlos do?

I have a confession to make. I have an imaginary friend named Carlos. He's actually not 100 percent imaginary; there really is a Carlos. He exists. However, I don't really know him all that well, and in my mind I've probably blown him up to be way more mythically ideal than he actually is. To me, though, this guy just "gets it," so I now use my created version of Carlos as a guide.

Carlos wouldn't have had that last drink last night. Carlos has the self-control to say no.

Carlos would not have skipped the morning track workout.

Carlos doesn't care about your watch, car, or house.

Carlos would never apologize by text; he'd look you in the eye.

When shit happens, I ask myself, "What would Carlos do?"

We all have a Carlos, that guy who just seems to move through life with grace.

On the other side, we also have "that friend." The guy that your wife doesn't like. He's the first one you call when you get a free night and wanna blow off some steam.

He's the guy you work out with but really don't see much outside the gym.

He's the long-distance friend who always takes your side because he's not around to see or hear anyone else's side of the story. That makes it easy to accept your bullshit as gospel.

He's that person who only calls you so that he can drone on about himself for twenty minutes, never asks a single thing about you or your family, and then invariably as soon as you get a chance to talk says, "Have to jump, just got another call."

He's the one who asks and pretends to care about your opinion . . . only to make the exact opposite decision time and again.

Especially now at our age, there are lots of decisions and choices every day—career, marriage, faith, family, finances, health—where you get to consult Carlos or "that friend" when it comes to writing your next episode.

Claim your story

Remember our friends that came over last night? I asked my friend what he liked to drink.

Bourbon, he said.

I don't drink bourbon. When I drink, it's tequila.

Am I gonna serve him tequila?

No, he doesn't want that, and I'm not a selfish ass.

Am I going to try and convince him that tequila is better? No. I'm simply going to buy the best bottle of bourbon I can and serve it to him. I will drink my tequila. We're both happy. We both got what we wanted. This is not hard . . . right?

Why does it matter so much in many areas of our lives that we not only get what we want but that we also want others to want what we want? Why do we spend extra time and energy trying to win someone over so they see it our way?

Carlos would not waste his time trying to convince you of anything. He would just live his life, lead by example, and be true to himself.

So now, because I missed my morning workout, my Epsom salt bath, and my stretching appointment, I'm just gonna man the fuck up (because that's what Carlos would do and it's what my wife is "asking" me to do) and go clean out the garage for the next three hours.

I'll do what I can today and live to fight tomorrow. No bitching and moaning, no regrets, no taking the hammer to myself in punishment.

I've got another workout, a stay-at-home date night, and a full slate of appointments scheduled tomorrow, and I know I've got the drive to maximize my results in all those areas.

That's my story . . . and I'm sticking to it.

Reminders

Meditate. Practice gratitude. Breathe.

Don't overextend yourself.

Get more sleep.

Eliminate comparison.

Develop a uniform.

Call, don't text.

Mornings over evenings.

Help others.

Read a little more, watch a little less.

Let things play out.

Don't fuck with things that don't move the needle.

Be intentional.

The Third F
FINANCE

- [ ] Are you comfortable with your bank balance?
- [ ] How much would it take for you to retire right now?
- [ ] How much would it take for you to quit your job and do something else?
- [ ] Do you live to work or work to live?
- [ ] Would you turn a hobby into a business? Should you?
- [ ] What's your relationship with money?
- [ ] Do you have a life coach, advisor, or mentor, financial or otherwise?
- [ ] Do you have life insurance and a will?
- [ ] Whom do you talk to about where to invest your money?

CHAPTER 13

One-Eighty Your Life

**Change what you're doing if you want
to change your results.**

*In 2017, a week before Christmas, I got let go from my CFO
position at a restaurant group doing $20 million a year in
sales. I was not living to my fullest potential. It got me to the
point where one week before Christmas, I was let go. I had no
money in my bank account. We were a family of four then.
I had an eight-month-old baby, my wife, and kids. I just remember crying in my Honda Civic—pretty shitty car for a
CFO—I was lost, man. I was totally lost. Thankfully, when
you hit rock bottom, that's when you start paying attention
to the things you need to pay attention to. I like to say that's
the day I woke up. A great philosopher once said that every
human being has two lives. The second one starts when you
figure out you've only got one life. Crying in that car, not
knowing how I was going to feed my family and pay my rent,*

I decided from that day forward I was going to do something about it. It was either go completely rock bottom and give up, or make some changes. So that's what I did.

The first thing that I did even before I put myself in that position was start working on myself and my mindset. I listened to a podcast starting in October 2017 called The MF-CEO Project podcast that was introduced to me by my brother. I can still remember the first few episodes, Andy Frisella—he's a huge influence on my life—speaking to me about just getting shit done and speaking up for what you believe and always doing the right thing. That began the process of self-improvement. But I was at a point in my life where I didn't have the base. People say, "Follow your dreams, do what you want, become an entrepreneur." I was not in position to do any of that because I had put myself there. I was a nine-to-fiver. I managed the budget of a restaurant group doing $20 million, and I couldn't manage my own home budget. I felt like an imposter, and you could tell. I was overweight. I wasn't doing the things to help myself be a better person so I could be a better father, husband, team member. So that was the first thing I did when I found myself in that situation: asked myself what do I need to do make myself better. I began reading more. I began to gain access to free content on YouTube. I began to do affirmations on a daily basis. There's this one baseball-related motivational video that I listened to every day for six months, but it's Denzel Washington. It was one of those speeches that had the biggest impact on me. It kept me motivated.

What do I do now? I don't have a job. I don't know what the hell I'm going to do. First thing I did was apply for unemployment. Four hundred fifty dollars a week. I know with that I can at least afford some groceries and put some money *toward rent. I began to strictly budget our household expenses, cut back on anything that I could, and I also applied for a catering gig. I worked the catering job on weekends for about six months to help sustain my family. Eventually I found a job selling food trucks, which is what led me to where we are today.*

My wife was super supportive from the moment she found out. I am so glad that I was able to find this path with her. She has stuck with me through the ups and downs. She basically said, "We're going to get through this together. Do what you have to do." I had to borrow $750 from my sister for Christmas after getting fired, and I had to borrow $2,000 from my father-in-law to pay rent in January. It was very humbling. My ego was shot, but I vowed I would never leave my family's fate in the hands of others ever again.

— **PATRICK BOLANOS,** chief dreaming officer, Trailer King
Builders, a company that builds customized food
trucks, on *The Midlife Male* podcast,
Episode #133

* * *

Coming to terms with the steps for getting unstuck in your life when you're near rock bottom is tough. You may find your "why" in the process—in fact, that is an important first step—but implementing the "how" is a bitch. You may not feel like you have the capacity or resources to get in the game when you've put yourself in a position way at the end of the bench.

But here's the deal: similar to finding your "why," your "this" or sometimes even your "these" are personal and often known only to you. Often, the financial downfall is what slaps us across the face that there is a problem, but "this" and "these" come in many forms, and often rock bottom in one precipitates rock bottom in other areas. There's causation, and there's correlation. Usually in these situations, there's some of both.

"This" and "these" are the things you know you shouldn't be doing, the people you know you shouldn't be seeing, the foods you know you shouldn't be eating, the places you know you shouldn't be going . . . you get the idea.

Perhaps it's the group of "friends" you've been hanging around for years, yet you know are holding you back.

Or family members whose level of toxicity causes you pain and anxiety.

You work in a restaurant that makes and serves nothing but unhealthy foods while you're desperately trying to change your lifestyle. You've got a drinking problem, and yet you still follow your buddies to the bar twice a week.

You've set new goals and are changing as a person—growing, striving, and challenging yourself—but you're still doing the same things with the same people, going to the same places, and expecting different results. There's a word for this: failure.

Your list could be a long one or a short one, but you've got to get real with yourself about your "this" and "these." You've got to know the challenges you're facing and draw the line to yourself. Remind yourself often, and ask trusted friends to hold you accountable. When you're in a familiar situation, you'll be equipped to choose more wisely.

Hey, I still do it too. Far less than I used to, but I still come out of a meeting, an event, or something I "needed" to do for that person who constantly asks (we all have that guy!), and I'm like, "Never again. Why in the world did I say yes to that?"

Change is hard.

Saying no is difficult. Establishing boundaries and personal space may not feel natural. It's uncomfortable to get uncomfortable.

But the alternative is worse.

To break the cycle, you've got to reduce or eliminate what's holding you back. You've got to untether that enormous weight you've been carrying around so that you can move forward, faster.

If you're going to 180 your life, results aren't going to happen overnight, and you have to commit to the difficulties that come with the change. You didn't wake up one day living an inauthentic life; that happened as a near-death experience by a million cuts, my friend. Gaining your self-esteem and your true self requires mending at least a million times.

Get Curious

Five tips to help you get unstuck

1. **Give up the "all-or-nothing" attitude.**

   Most of the time, you don't have to think of your changes or progress as all-or-nothing. If it's certain "friends" or foods, just set an exception for a cheat day every once in a while. Over time, you'll most likely come to the realization that your desire to cheat is waning.

2. **Let it go.**

    Stuff happens to everybody, and everyone you meet is fighting their own personal battles. The worst thing you can do is not let it go. By not letting go of the past, our lives become increasingly more difficult. Some things are not in our control; don't let that consume you from achieving your goals. Remember, most people aren't thinking about you at all; they're too busy thinking about themselves.

3. **Write it down.**

    Write down what you want to do, where, with whom, how. The more details, the better. Then— and this is the important part—refer to it *before* you respond to any requests, emails, calls, or conversations that could derail you. It's easy to write down goals. Write down your "outs" too. Keep a list of responses to politely and respectfully get you out of doing the things and saying yes to the things that will keep you from reaching your goals.

4. **Surround yourself with good people.**

    If you surround yourself with people who are go-getters, passionate and smart about what they do, then those qualities will rub off on you. Take the time to audit your group of friends, your coworkers and work environment, and even your family. If these people are not contributing to your life in a healthy, positive way, reconsider how much time you spend with them.

5. **Exercise.**

   A common thread among great minds is exercise. Whether it's a sport, going to the gym, or even taking a brisk walk through the park, being in tune with your body will help you get through the mental marathons required to produce great work.

Coaching Options Are Everywhere

Everything you need to help you be successful is available to you twenty-four hours a day, seven days a week, and for free.

The absolute best and the brightest in the world make themselves accessible through various media, posts, webinars, and Zoom conferences, and now we're seeing the world opening back up again to in-person events.

I take advantage of as many of these opportunities as I can.

This morning I registered for a free seminar with the Weitz Effect. Personal style is important to me and something I'm passionate about. So when Tom Brady's stylist is offering a free seminar focused on exactly what I want to learn about, you're damn right I'm gonna sign up.

I kicked my training off this morning with a workout that Coach Sam Tooley posted. Sam won the Hyrox America fitness competition. I'd like to win Hyrox (I actually just want to survive Hyrox), so why wouldn't I experiment with a program that has a proven track record of success?

I could go on about finance, food, family, and anything you're interested in learning about and improving on, but here's the kicker . . . all this free, excellent content is great, but it's not enough.

Despite the availability of a wealth of free content and expertise, the reason I still consistently use coaches is for accountability. I also require communication and need someone to push me on curiosity, responsibility, stimulation, motivation, and inspiration, and to call me on bullshit.

It's so I'm able to go from knowing what to do to actually doing what I need to do.

It's to help me take the things in my head from idea to execution.

It's also why aggregating credible content, service providers, experts, resources, and products is such a big part of what I do on the podcast, the newsletter, and in my own coaching practice.

This is what I am actually doing for myself. It's what my coaches are doing for me.

I use coaches because I can't do it all on my own. The reason people use me is because they can't do it on their own either. If we all could, we would.

We're just paying it forward.

CHAPTER 14

"Better One? Or Two?"

Be willing to ask questions.

I used to be that way where I'm going to read all these things and become the most optimized person. I was the self-development jackass type. Fortunately, I've worked with some coaches who have helped me tone that down, and I've realized what Oprah says, that you can only run your own race. That's really what I want to focus on with me and also my clients: What does a win look like to you as opposed to what somebody else wants? One person might want six-pack abs, and the other person might just want to be thin. Some people might want to make a million dollars, and the other person is like, I'm cool with 200K as long as I've got more free time to spend with my family and I have peace of mind. That's what I try to dial in on more and more. What fulfills me as opposed to what do I think I should do based on what I see other people doing?

For me, I need time. I need space away from social media to think and figure out what I really need. What I see with a lot of guys is that they're really busy, they work a lot, and then they fill their time with all these things, whether it's social media or TV or sports or whatever it is. They don't have any time to really think about, "What is a 'Hell, yeah!' life for me? How can I create that?"

It's really easy to fall back into old habits and routines. The lockdown might have been good for some people. It's a big shake-up. I see this in people who go through a big change in their life. September 11 made people reconsider some things. When people go through a divorce or something like that, that's when people wonder, "Oh, what am I doing with my life, and maybe I'm going at it the wrong way, and maybe I should do something differently." That's the point when I love meeting people, because they're open and their ready for change.

— **JON MITCHELL,** functional medicine practitioner, physician assistant, and health consultant, on *The Midlife Male* podcast, Episode #117

* * *

"Better one? Or two?"

You know the drill. Every time you go to the optometrist for a checkup, he or she does that little test where they flip around the lenses and say, "Better one? Or two?" and keep doing this over and over one eye at a time until they get your prescription right. Then at the end, they reveal both eyes, and you read the letters back in full clarity.

When I visit the eye doctor, it gets me thinking that this process is a lot like life: in business, family, fitness, finance, and pretty much everything we experience, we try, fail, succeed, do, try again, fail, succeed, try again, and on and on. Ultimately, we navigate our way through until we gain focus and clarity. For some of us, this comes as quickly as the eye exam; for others of us, it takes years. Some may never get the vision they desire.

I didn't join Insgroup until I was thirty-seven. I didn't become an athlete until forty. I didn't start my podcast until I was forty-five. In my twenties, I was a mess, and now, nearing fifty, I know that my life is still just beginning.

I've been flipping lenses for more than twenty years: "Better *one* or *two*," figuring it out as I go. I just may finally have the right prescription:

- I prefer mornings and daytime to nighttime.
- I feel better not drinking than drinking.
- I like watching movies, not producing them.
- I'm having more fun working out at different places than when I owned a gym.
- I'm a better servant for others than I am for myself.
- I prefer . . .

  staying in to going out.

  reading magazines and articles over books.

  being free to being in an office.

  collaborating over selling.

  being creative and flexible over rigid and overly structured.

doing over watching.

producing content versus consuming it.

I'm passionate about entrepreneurs, fitness, food, products, and lifestyle, and in business and in life, I'm fortunate that I get to engage in each of those areas every day. That's taken a lot of time and experience to realize that it's actually possible to combine your personal passions with professional expertise. For years, I thought work was work and play was play. I didn't get the notion that if you do what you love, you'll never work a day in your life.

With the podcast, I started to interview extraordinary men so I could learn and be inspired. Needless to say, the process has helped me to grow, figure out who I am, what I enjoy, define my purpose, gain confidence, make friends, and develop new relationships.

The more recent phase of my life is asking myself how I can continue to move forward and take my business and personal brand to the next level by serving others and helping them get better and improve their lives.

Can you make the ask?

If you follow journalist Dave Meltzer, you know he proposes to ask two simple questions of at least one new person every day:

1. How may I serve you?

2. Do you know anybody that can help me?

Everything is based on your network, relationships, referrals, and connections, so these seem like valuable, straightforward questions.

So why is it so hard to make the ask? Or should I say, why is it hard to make the ask for some things and not others?

- I find it easy to ask guys to come on the podcast but hard to ask them for their business.
- I find it hard to ask for things for myself but easy to advocate for my clients and friends.
- I find it easy to ask guys to meet me for a workout/ breakfast but hard to ask for an office meeting.

Is where we feel most comfortable—the easier ask? What environments give us confidence? Which situations feel most authentic? Why do we struggle with asking?

I don't have all the answers. However, I do know that I've flipped the lenses a lot in these areas. When I feel comfortable and am in an environment that energizes me and in situations where I'm surrounded by like-minded people with similar interests and passions, I do well. When I step outside this, I don't.

It's a constant process to get comfortable being uncomfortable. You have to keep asking questions—of yourself *and* others. That's how you stay open to change. That's how you create your own style, set your own priorities, and seek the opportunities that mean something to you.

Even before the pandemic, Kate and I were kind of outliers in that we didn't necessarily want to attend every happy hour or golf outing or obligatory function. We weren't trying to be lame; we were just trying to simplify our lives.

During the pandemic, we were no longer the outliers because these things didn't exist for anyone.

As the world opened up again, we have had to ask ourselves, "What do we want in our lives?"

Are we being intentional in our choices? Are we making the ask?

* * *

It's been nearly two decades since I had Lasik surgery, and I'm finally seeing a slight deterioration in my vision. Kate actually gave me "the gift of sight" for my thirtieth birthday. It was either that or a watch. "Better one? Or two?"

I question a lot of my life decisions; this was one where I definitely made the right choice.

None of us always makes the right choice, but as we get older, we see many things with greater clarity—it's one of the perks of middle age. I certainly hope I see the high-priority things better (specifically, the six Fs in this book) and make better decisions related to them.

We still don't have perfect vision. That's why asking the questions of ourselves and others is so important.

"Better one? Or two?"

"1. How may I serve you?"

"2. Do you know anybody who can help me?"

And by the way, don't be surprised if you get a call from me with a couple of questions.

Get in the Right Room

In business and in life, we should always strive to surround ourselves with people who are fitter, smarter, and more successful. That's how we improve. That's how we ensure success.

If I'm the fittest, smartest, or "best" at anything in the room, then I'm in the wrong fucking room.

You don't become more successful in your business by thinking you know it all already. My partners are smarter than me. My clients are smarter than me. I'm just smart enough to appreciate that they still let me learn from them.

Always seek out opportunities for improvement, mentorship, guidance, and expertise from those out ahead. And if those people are willing to share their time with you, any time at all, you'd be foolish not to take it.

If you don't take it, that's just pure ego and insecurity doing the talking for you.

Navigating middle age to achieve a better quality of life means being willing to be vulnerable, humble, and proactive.

When you're open to doing things differently, you can figure out what's working and what's not, who's working in your life and who's not. That's when you can make the tweaks necessary to become better and happier.

CHAPTER 15
Following Only Your Passion Is a Cop-Out

Keep your day job *and* follow your dreams.

Something clicks eventually. At some point, you have to stop chasing just what you want. I wanted to write movies. I had a couple screenplays out there. That writers' strike hit in '08, and for me that changed my life in a very specific way because I had put everything in that pot of the rainbow of, I'm just going to freelance and do this other stuff. But when I sell my big screenplay for six figures or something, then I'm going to be able to do what I want. It's a terrible way to live, and I'm sure every twenty-year-old does it. But I actually had a deal with New Line Cinema for this script. It was what I wanted. No joke, I remember sitting in this meeting with this manager who had been working with me, it was the production company that did Wedding Crashers. *It was a perfect fit. And the* offer was really good—not life changing, but it would take the pressure off for a while. And the guy says, "Look, this is all contingent on the strike that is going to happen in about a month. If the strike doesn't happen, the project's a go. If not, then I can't promise anything, because I don't know where it's going to be."

You remember the strike. It was like a year. And I realized I put all my happiness in these other people's hands. I put all my financial future in this other company's hands. What a dumbass! I need to work! And literally, six months later, I was back on staff at Muscle Fitness. I was working for Flex again. From that point on, I've always had an anchor. That's when I realized that what I wanted to do is build this career. Write books, ghostwrite books, copywrite, make a living doing this instead of hoping that I could put it together until I sold the screenplay.

People who do anything creative for a living—funny enough—as freewheeling as we like to think we are, are extremely stubborn. We just want to do what we want to do. I am beyond guilty. I still struggle with this at times . . . When I woke up from that moment in '08, what I realized is you can chase anything, but you've got to have an anchor of some kind for financial security and responsibility. I'm at Muscle Fitness, I'm at Men's Fitness. I'm in this world where I want to be in. Do I enjoy interviewing for the seventeenth time the "biceps grow two inches on your arm summer workout" article? No! It's the same thing. I've written that seventeen times. But you're moving up the masthead. You're becoming a senior editor. Your salary's getting better. You're contributing. Then in the off time, that's when I realized I want to write books. There's so few authors that make a living writing books. It's *like 0.001 percent. You have to have the anchor. As you get older, the books get bigger and bigger, and the paydays get bigger, and maybe you option a few things, but at the end of the day there's an anchor to keep you rolling so that there's not so much pressure on every book deal or whatever you're doing as an entrepreneur. If you can get a stream of income doing something, it takes the pressure off the moonshots.*

— **JON FINKEL,** author of *1996: A Biography, Hoops Heist, The Life of Dad, Jocks in Chief, The Athlete,* and more, on *The Midlife Male* podcast, Episode #148

* * *

People ask me all the time, "What do you do for a living?" They think I'm in the fitness or nutrition industries. No, I'm not. My anchor for more than fifteen years was the insurance business. Was it sexy? Not as sexy as what I post on Instagram. But I realized my days of operating without a safety net were over. If you're a Midlife Male—or future Midlife Male—reading this book, hear me out on this one.

I get paid quite a lot of money to work out, host a podcast, write a newsletter, try amazing products, work with tremendous people and brands, and have a lot of quality time on my hands.

That's why I didn't quit my job, throw caution to the wind, and follow my "passion" until I was in a financial position to take the leap. There is no perfect. Doing nothing more than continually following your passions is a cop-out and can lead to a pretty unfulfilling existence.

Now before you go saying I settled, was miserable, compromising, selling myself short, missing out, or will one day be on my deathbed feeling regretful, let me tell you that's complete bullshit.

I have followed *all* of my passions. Still do.

An *anchor* is not a bad thing unless you think it is. An anchor keeps the boat from floating off to BFE. And the captain controls the anchor. You, my friend, are the captain. Act like one.

A more responsible and impressive feat is not quitting your job. Instead, do it better and better, and find opportunities to scratch whatever itch you have in the process or in your off time. That's what I've created for myself, and it makes me healthier and happier, and I've gotten better results.

My twenties

In my twenties, I produced movies. *Two Ninas*, with the amazing Amanda Peet, Ron Livingston, and Cara Buono, won numerous festivals and helped several of the stars continue working upward in their craft. You can find it on Amazon and Netflix now. Check it out! It holds up. *Boricua's Bond* starred Method Man, Tyson Beckford, Big Pun, Treach, Onyx, and more. Not exactly great, but we sold it to USA Films.

I had produced a couple others and moved down to South Beach to work for The Shooting Gallery, a production company that was best known for Billy Bob Thornton's early movies. Within a couple years in Miami, I had determined my passion wasn't in film. (In fact, I rarely watch any movies or TV anymore.) I chose to move on from it, though a brainstorm I had a few years later used my production skills.

My thirties

Pairing my dad hat and my film hat, I went full entrepreneur.

I realized that when I was at home with our firstborn, Auden, I was watching mind-numbing amounts of *Sesame Street*, *Baby Einstein*, and the like, wishing I could be watching ESPN instead. (Don't tell me you haven't done the same, you dads reading this.) I figured I could marry these various interests and came up with a line of sports and baby videos. Team Baby Entertainment was born!

I used my experience in production to create a series of children's videos that emulated *Baby Einstein* but utilized the footage, mascots, colors, shapes, numbers, and athletes from college and professional teams. I was the first person to license actual game footage for the purposes of children's home entertainment.

I grew the company from selling hastily produced sports-themed DVDs out of the trunk of my car to a $10-million-plus valuation and deals with the NBA, MLB, and NCAA. I was featured on Donnie Deutsch's TV show and in the *New York Times*. We were written up in every publication you could think of, and I made numerous TV appearances, including on the Home Shopping Network.

Michael Eisner, former CEO of Disney, invested in the company, and I ultimately sold it to him. He helped me grow it and have some of the top celebrities in the world as our narrators. It was a blast matching A-listers with their teams: Matthew McConaughey and the University of Texas. Regis Philbin and Notre Dame. Mark Cuban and the Mavs. Ben Affleck and the Red Sox. I even got to go to Tampa Bay to record George Steinbrenner reading the script for our beloved New York Yankees.

We imploded in a few years when the DVD market went in the crapper and pediatricians started telling parents that putting your kid in front of the TV to watch *Baby Einstein* or our videos was not such a great idea after all. I made hokey sports videos, was on the road all the time at trade shows, markets, vendors, and campuses, and was doing press and marketing constantly. I completely missed the mark on the transition of hard goods (DVDs) to apps/online/streaming; I wasn't prepared to change my whole business model.

Eisner moved on to bigger things. Team Baby went bust. Perhaps if I had better vision, it would have led to a bigger payday down the line and a more expansive business to run. My life might have gone any number of directions.

Not that I'm complaining. It was an incredible ride, and I made a decent chunk of change. I certainly try not to have regrets, and I have enjoyed the other ventures I've had through the years. I'm pretty sure greater success might have made me an even bigger asshole than I was at the time.

Personally, I was dealing with a lot. I was a husband and father. My grandmother (my father's mother, whom I adored and was extremely close to) had just died. My brother was arrested and ultimately sent to prison for five years. My mother was suffering from some serious mental and emotional issues. Baggage . . . lots of it, and I wasn't really dealing with it well. But juggling shit is part of what we have to do when we're figuring out our place in life.

My forties

Later, I opened ROW Studios to turn my love of fitness into a business. Five years of sweat, lost friendships, and lost money, and I was out.

When I opened the gym, I was in the best shape of my life. But I could never quite figure out the model, get aligned with my partners, and manage the team properly. When I sold it, I was in the worst shape I'd been in in ten years, physically and mentally.

Not everybody can handle success in their twenties and thirties without losing their soul. I'm quite certain the Universe knew what it was doing with me by giving me challenges back then.

In my late forties now, I want enough money to provide me the freedom to have the lifestyle I want, and not a penny more. It's not worth it to me to work my ass off to be trapped at my desk trying to become a billionaire. I'm happy to let my money work for me while I'm pursuing what I think is fun. I haven't actually been very good at any of the things I was passionate about when it came to making them viable businesses. More importantly, I certainly wasn't all that happy with all the added pressures and responsibilities I was taking on.

In between Team Baby and ROW, I made a wiser career decision and joined Insgroup. I did my own personal SWOT analysis. When I considered my strengths, weaknesses, successes, and failures, I thought about what I had learned and what I still wanted to learn, the type of service I wanted to provide, and the value I felt I could bring.

Most importantly, I thought about the types of clients I wanted to represent and the types that I felt would want someone to represent them with my experience, skill set, passion, and commitment to ensuring success in business and in life.

I factored in longevity, sustainability, quality of life, risk versus reward, recurring revenue, the lifestyle I wanted to live, the lifestyle I wanted to be able to provide for my family, and other criteria.

At the time, everyone I knew seemed to have an opinion on what I was doing.

"What? You're gonna go sell insurance now? You were on *The Big Idea* last year. You were Michael Eisner's partner. You were producing films with Harvey Weinstein *before* he was a pariah."

Yeah, but I wasn't happy, wasn't really making life-changing money, didn't have any consistency or discipline, and came to the realization that no matter what your passion and interests are, work is very much still work. Nothing is glamorous.

What's real is that:

* Residual income is a great thing.

* Being able to work with anyone I want is exciting.

* Having something to offer that everyone has to have is a whole lot better than trying to sell something that nobody needs.

- Building a book of business is better than owning a business and all the headaches that come along with it.
- Doing good work for good people is satisfying.

Every industry, office, system, business, and culture is fucked up to a certain degree. It's just how you see it and respond to it and perform in it that matters.

Money buys freedom; discipline equals freedom

Have both.

If I told you that you could make [insert your magic dollar amount here] working out and hosting a podcast, would you take it?

Now what if I told you that you had to work for ten-plus years to build that book of business that creates that kind of revenue in order to get it?

Would you still do it?

And that you'd have to put in ten, twenty, sometimes fifty hours a week to maintain it and even grow it?

Would you do it then?

I know why you want to host the show, take the pictures, follow your passion, travel, exercise, and be influential, but pay attention to the part about "how" you'll be able to do it.

If you're a member of the lucky sperm club and blessed to be born into money, then you don't need any of the advice I'm giving. But if you're like most of us, you have to figure it out.

Trying to turn my hobbies and passions into businesses is no longer my goal.

Making my business work for my passions has yielded far greater results.

Insuring the fitness company I love is more gratifying and more lucrative than starting one up.

The hospitality group, tortilla chip brand, men's grooming product line . . . I can be a part of it all now. And that's actually really impactful.

I get to go visit, be a part of their professional service team, and then leave all the pressures of entrepreneurship and "owning" a business to their founder.

That's why those guys get the big bucks. And only after years of working their asses off to become an overnight success. Success and a payout are never guaranteed, and failure is almost always the ending.

Instead, through consistency and combining personal passion with professional expertise, I've been able to build something of value.

Not without struggle, compromise, frustrations, and the "grass is greener" feelings that creep back in frequently. But I have no business overhead, no team to manage, no investors to report to.

I've been able to pick up some equity along the way, which is great as we've tripled in size since I joined, and I'd never want to trade places with our CEO or top producers. I accept that they do the heavy lifting and I just do my job. That's fair.

And as a result, I'm very well compensated and get to be of service, do good work for great clients, host a podcast with amazing guests, work out a lot, and spend time with my family.

Don't only follow your passion. Make it one part of your decision-making process.

I know I make better financial and life decisions now. In so many ways, I see the Universe offering me opportunities each and every day now.

I say, "Bring it on, Universe!" You can trust me with your money, and I'll be happy to pay it forward.

You Do You (Are You Listening to Him?)

I'm not someone who does particularly well with change.

I eat mostly the same foods, maintain a set schedule, have the same wife forever, keep a tight circle of real friends.

Routine, discipline, and consistency are my things, and materially, I find myself needing less and focusing more on curating quality-over-quantity items that improve my life, don't add stress or overhead, and shorten my runway.

I'm curious by nature and question everything.

How much money is enough?

Do you love what you do?

Is there an opportunity to do something new?

Do you want or need to do anything at all?

Do you work to live or live to work?

Is balance even possible?

These questions come up a lot with guys that join me on the pod. A lot of these Midlife Males have experienced their exit or are working their asses off to get to theirs.

They've worked at something for a while, had success, and when they're able to take their chips off the table and get to that number (I guess everybody has a number), they move on to something else.

I'm also seeing a lot of these guys become coaches, mentors, and advisors, launch a podcast of their own, and get deep into health and wellness and recovery. It seems that there's this time period where they're making up for some of the dissatisfaction of their prior choices, the long hours of sacrifices, the things that have gone wrong with relationships because business was all too consuming, and they're trying to capture happiness now because they have the financial freedom to do so.

And there are certainly a lot of others that, even when their "exit" comes or the acquisition is there, they don't see it as the end or even a new beginning.

They just go right back to work. Tomorrow looks a lot like yesterday.

Maybe they just love it: the art of the deal, the business, they can't get away, don't want to get up from behind the desk.

Perhaps they don't see anything wrong . . . and maybe there isn't anything wrong.

It's all about perspective, your personal view of the situation you're in and the situation you wish to create for your future.

CHAPTER 16

"Fuck Off, Harvey"

Be true to yourself.

After we had made Raw Deal *and certainly after* Cocaine Cowboys *in 2006, the entertainment industry was in the full throes of the reality television boom. Certainly,* Real World *came out in the '90s, but the year* Raw Deal *came out, 2001,* Survivor *premiered. There was* Big Brother *and* Keeping Up with the Kardashians *and* Real Housewives *around then. In 2006 and 2007, there were a lot of people trying to get us into the reality television business: You guys make documentaries; it's a short hop over here. There's a ton of money in it. You make these shows and then you format them and they make 150 episodes.*

I remember Billy [Corben], Dave [Cypkin], and I sitting down and entertaining some ideas and concepts. We said, you know, we don't watch reality television. I don't really know what makes one show good or one show bad. To me, it was all kind of television wallpaper. It didn't interest us, and it wasn't something we would want to watch. Probably pigheadedly, we said we're not going to do that. We're going to stay in our lane making premium documentaries, which was not the way to go if you wanted to cash in. It was still a struggle for a while after Cocaine Cowboys, because making feature documentaries was not a real business for a very long time. We started to get some commissions. Thankfully, ESPN launched 30 for 30 in the midst of the Great Recession, which we always called the full employment program for documentary filmmakers. Thank God to the ESPN folks, because they put all of us to work in 2008 and '09 and '10 and '11.

But then something peculiar happened. The Jinx hit on HBO. Making a Murderer hit on Netflix. All of a sudden, the multipart premium documentaries were a thing. And now, because of Netflix and Amazon and Hulu, there were more avenues than ever to distribute premium documentary content. What the entertainment industry eventually realized was that there was a huge pent-up demand for premium nonfiction storytelling that was never being addressed in the marketplace because the marketplace was dictated by ten to twelve channels at the time or maybe four to five acquisitions executives. Netflix, with its unlimited shelf space, exposed that. At Blockbuster, there's only so many slots for DVDs, but on Netflix you have unlimited shelf space. People were finally offered a plethora of options, and the marketplace was allowed to dictate what the popular content was that we would be talking about at the watercooler. In our business, what has unfolded in the past five or six years is fascinating. The pendulum has swung to premium documentaries, and I think it's going to stay there because people like to watch nonfiction and finally the marketplace has woken up to it.

— **ALFRED SPELLMAN,** cofounder/producer, rakontur, on *The Midlife Male* podcast, Episode #136

* * *

There's an economics lesson to be learned here, but the takeaway may not be as cut and dried as you might think.

When you're a Midlife Male, it rarely is.

When I moved to Miami in 1999, I met Alfred and Billy. Alfred tells me the rakontur guys looked at me as someone to emulate since I had a modicum of success in the industry in which they were young, ambitious, and striving to make an impact. But telling stories was in their blood. I knew a thing or two about producing movies, but I was ready to be out of that world soon after I got there.

Kudos to rakontur. They stuck with their plan even when the marketplace wasn't aligned to their interests. That's not always a good call, but they knew what they loved and what they were about when it came to their creative choices and process. Even if they had bombed, you would have to credit them for staying true to themselves.

My opportunity to stay true to myself happened when I was still in New York. It didn't have to do with my content creation but rather my dignity. My first job out of college was with Miramax, as an assistant to Harvey Weinstein. Looking in from the outside at that time, that seemed like I had been given the ball under the basket. All I had to do was dunk it home.

Perception and reality are not always the same, however.

Day in and day out, I saw how he treated people, men and women. And I saw how people, men and women, were desperate to take meetings with him. I never saw him do anything illegal, but I saw him berate and bully, bitch and moan, and most of the time, I saw him get his way. I wanted a future in film, but after almost two years, I couldn't escape what my dad was surely saying as he rolled over in his grave: "Greg, don't let anyone talk to you this way." That was really the extent of my consideration, and eventually I had enough.

"Fuck off, Harvey," I said. And I left.

He called me back in a day or so, not exactly apologizing on the voice mail but letting me know I had showed him and I should come back since I had had my fun. He was patronizing as fuck. I never talked to him again.

I went to Miami after telling Harvey to fuck off. Not necessarily easy to do when you're trying to build a career and your boss is the kingmaker. Unfortunately, he was an even bigger asshole and sexual predator than he was a film mogul.

Here's what I learned from that brush with trash: Dad was right. We shouldn't let people talk to others like that. If we as a society didn't allow people to talk to others like that, it wouldn't give those people license to get away with bullying and much, much worse.

Houston, we have a father

Pursuing your passion sounds easy when you see it on inspirational posters and Insta feeds. It's not as easy when you're in the thick of the shit, and you need to provide for yourself and others.

Providing. That is a helluva lot more motivation than pursuing some ill-defined passion.

Kate and I met when I was still living in Miami. But soon we moved to her hometown of Houston. This was good for me; by that point I'd had enough of New York City and Miami.

This was a blow to my still-fragile male ego though. When we got to Houston, I didn't really know anybody besides Kate. I had no job, no connections, and not a whole lot of money. I figured we could sustain ourselves for about two years before I really needed to figure something out. All I knew at the time was entertainment, film, and being a wannabe hotshot producer. There was nothing like that in Houston.

I got a job at the local TV station because I thought that was the closest thing to entertainment I could be involved in. It was boring as hell, but somehow they found a creative slot for me, and over time I was able to create some nontraditional revenue opportunities for the station.

I became the number one salesperson there, and that got me recruited by a larger television group, so I moved across town to work for them and continued to move up. I still knew that this was not personally or professionally satisfying, but we had our first child, Auden, and then a second, Harper.

Providing. Did I mention that is another word for motivation?

I was in a weird spot. I had launched Team Baby Entertainment, which gave me national attention because of my high-profile partnership with Eisner and presumption of success. But I still didn't know anybody in Houston and wasn't confident I would get anybody in town to talk to me.

In figuring out my next move, I did what any creative producer would do: I created a television show to interview people that I wanted to learn from and get to know. If you bring a camera, people like to talk about themselves and be on TV, right? So that's what I did.

I cold-called some of Houston's best and brightest and told them I had a television show called *PROFILE* where I was going to interview the top entrepreneurs and risk-takers in our city. I invited them to come on the show. Nobody even to be bothered to ask when it was on and what channel it was on; they just all said yes.

Next, I went to Houston PBS, because I figured no other station would give me a time. Plus, public broadcasting sounded free and the path of least resistance and more intellectually stimulating. I told the program director at PBS that I had a thirty-minute talk show featuring the brightest people in Houston, and all I needed from them was thirty minutes' worth of airtime each week for me to deliver them a finished product.

They jumped at the opportunity. I don't think they believed me, but they jumped anyway. So now I had a time slot, guests, and a show to produce. We did twenty-four episodes of that show, and I felt like I met everyone in town during that time.

Halfway through recording episodes of *PROFILE*, I met the team from Insgroup. We discussed my joining their insurance and risk management firm, and I accepted.

This was the most conservative and professional thing I'd ever done in my life. Strangely, that is what petrified me. But I sensed there was an opportunity to build something special and have a stable and scalable career.

I would be a responsible grown-up for once and have some security, recurring revenue, and a future with an actual viable product and service that people and businesses needed.

Up until then, nothing I had ever been involved with had been anything that anyone actually needed. I negotiated a deal in which if I had successful metrics and hit some numbers, then I would have the opportunity to buy into the firm. This became significant.

Money, passion, or both?

Meanwhile, I have lived in Houston for nearly two decades and have transferred my love of meeting the best and brightest to a weekly podcast. I tell my own story through social media and a weekly newsletter. I know incredible people all over the Houston metropolitan area and around the country and the world.

I'm not sure if I'm aiming bigger, and I don't really care. I just know I'm aiming at what I want and with far more precision.

So what do you think about this question?

If I gave you an amount of money with the stipulation that you could never work again, what would the amount be? And what would you do from then on? Could you do it?

I hate that old adage, "If you have a job you love, then you never have to work a day in your life." Is there really anything that you can be so passionate about that it doesn't feel like work after you've been doing it awhile?

I attended the Natural Foods Show in Anaheim a few years back because I insure several of the companies that were there and am always looking for new clients, prospects, and ideas. I like to eat, drink, and work out, so I've chosen to focus on insuring those types of brands, businesses, and entrepreneurs. It feels more "right" to me to be able to combine my personal passions and experiences with my professional expertise. It took me a while to figure that out. In fact, I'm still figuring it out.

I saw all those people at the show . . . repping the brands, creating the brands, selling the brands, working the brands. Some were worth millions; others weren't making a dime. I saw really young, naive, energetic entrepreneurs, and I saw a guy with a walker still repping product even though it must've taken him two hours just to get in and out of the convention center each day.

How do you choose what you're going to do? Is it money or passion that drives you? Or does it really come down to simply "I choose to do 'this' so that I can afford to do 'that'?" Meaning, did you pick a career path for the upside of money so that you can have a huge house and take fancy vacations? Or did you follow your passion regardless of the financial "upside"?

If you think I'm trying to trick you into making the noble response here, you're wrong. There is no right answer.

Whatever your own personal "this" may be, wherever you decided to place your bet, does it really matter what you choose to do as much as that you just do it well? More than what you do, it's how you do it that matters for success.

As I walked through aisle after aisle of products at the show (seriously, how many protein bars, CBD products, MCT oils, and butter coffee brands can there be?! I am totally into all this shit, but seriously . . .), it became very clear to me that it's all about the people, not the product.

Who, not what

Who stood out to me mattered, not *what*. Nothing sells itself. I sold insurance for years. People are going to buy it from somebody. Why not me?

Who do you want to buy from? Who do you want to work with? That's everything right there.

People remember how you make them feel more than anything. Are you nice? Are you an expert? Are you both? It goes beyond the marketing, packaging, look, feel, style over substance. How are you going to cut through the clutter, make a statement, find your audience, and connect with people? Be more than a commodity; be something special. The further I get along in life, the more I realize that it is the value of relationships and being authentic that really drive true success and happiness.

Which brings us back to Harvey Weinstein and the economics lesson I mentioned at the start of this chapter. When he got arrested and stories kept pouring in about his actions, we heard a lot about how he could be successful being that way. The implication was that understanding the dynamics around him was complicated.

That's bullshit. I look back and think that leaving that job with Harvey was actually one of the easiest things I've ever done. I retained my dignity. I landed on my feet.

The guy was a bully and wielded incredible power. You could look at him and say he's proof that you don't have to stand out by treating people well and being a mensch, that decency doesn't result in "success." But let me ask you this. Even before his conviction, would you want to live with yourself every day the way Weinstein has to?

If you're a sociopath, maybe so. For the vast majority of us, we recognize there's more to life.

I'm not saying money isn't important. It may not buy love or happiness, but I don't have many problems that another $500,000 a year couldn't solve. That sounds shitty, but sorry/not sorry. Just don't equate your empathy and influence with your bank account. That's the economics lesson right there.

The BS and the bottom line of the "follow your passion" trope.

The guys at rakontur, they stuck with what they were passionate about, but they did it for sound reasons. They didn't go after something they didn't know about—and more importantly, didn't *care* to know anything about. I'm all for trying new things and getting out of your comfort zone. But you shouldn't do it just because you see it as a cash grab any more than you should be a narcissistic asshole just to retain control of other people. You get results either way, but at what cost?

Don't make yourself miserable grabbing the low-hanging fruit. Low-hanging fruit tastes good, but if you want to chase something that *you* think tastes better, go for it. In Alfred and Billy and Dave's case, it just so happens the higher branches also were more lucrative for their skills and their goals. I'm going to go out on a limb here—yeah,

I just made that pun—and say that more often than not, that's actually the case with all of us.

Follow your passion? OK, go for it. But do it with resolve and intelligence, and above all, keep your integrity. I can honestly say that on that front, I can sleep well at night knowing that I did what I needed to do back then . . . and still do.

Get What You Want, Not Just What You Need

I have everything I need.

I do not have everything I want.

I am grateful, appreciative, and happy for all that I have, yet I still want, aspire, and desire additional things to accomplish more and to help me, my family, and my clients live better lives and reach their goals.

Consider that both of these are perfectly OK.

It's not about the material, keep-up-with-the-Joneses or about the shiny objects themselves, but rather the experiences and value they add to achieving total life wellness. The desire for more does not necessarily have to mean piling up more possessions. There's a lot more to wanting and a lot less to needing than we often think.

Here are some of the things that are on my want list:

- Money. Finance 101 here: There are two ways to accumulate money. You either spend less or earn more. People don't like to talk about this, but money buys freedom. This should be a priority and not something to be embarrassed to put first. There are places I want to go and experiences I want us to have. As the family provider, that's on me. It's that simple.

- Beach house in Costa Rica. I'd love to have a place for our family. Something simple, clean, modern, and all ours.

- Midlife Male cliché here, but yeah . . . I want a sports car. Haven't had one since right after college. I'm thinking something iconic, classy, and black. Maybe a 911 or a Maserati (preowned, of course, with low miles).

- Trailer/camper. I really enjoy the road trips, day trips, and quality time of just "going places." Whether I'm with the wife and kids, dogs, bikes, friends, or alone, these experiences make memories that are healthy and can never be canceled. Also, bonus: could use this as an office, studio, or music lounge.

What's on your list?

CHAPTER 17

Your Job Doesn't Care about You

Get out of your work what you need.

I didn't graduate college and start a business right away. I had over five years [of experience] in the traditional workforce and learned quite a bit about how the corporate world worked and doing the standard learning about leadership in smaller groups as you mature in a company. I learned from some really great mentors, but I would say identifying people with the same values as me was the key. That's who I wanted to align myself with, and then I knew that with those people I could accomplish what I wanted to. It's a long arc from there to where I now have control of my schedule as a business owner. Starting off, there was definitely taking my lumps and working for someone for a number of years and a large learning curve when I had my own custom audiovisual business.

[In] my exit from audio/video into hospitality, where I had no direct experience, I was looking to what does the future

hold for this business? It's really easy and great to sell these TVs, and we're doing this big house and all these great things. But you kind of sensed what was coming down the road technologically. In the audio/video world, the Sonos speaker system and the iPhone made it very apparent to me that I couldn't in good conscience sell people five-dollar, ten-dollar, fifteen-thousand-dollar complicated audio/video systems that weren't going to do nearly as much as something that they could buy and hook up themselves. It was important to me that I stayed above board and said I need to feel good about what I'm doing and what I'm selling. At the same time, of course, I want to make some money at it. Neither of those things were aligning. It was clear that coming down the road that we weren't going to be needed. That was basically an exit strategy. I started reaching out to other companies I had worked with or had done some business with in our field and ultimately found a company that was interested in acquiring us, and that was the transition.

I was recently married, and I had kids on the way during this transition, so it was definitely somewhat a frightening time, but we were prepared for it. I'd been in business for a long time, and it was important to identify what I was passionate about, because as an entrepreneur you are going to be involved in it twenty-four seven. If you're not passionate about it, you've already lost.

— **JOE KROUSE,** owner of Ten Mile House, Fred's Garage, and DB3 Donuts, on *The Midlife Male* podcast, Episode #19

* * *

I'm not telling you to leave your job for a new career, and I'm not telling you to make the most out of your current job.

I'm not saying you need to tell the CEO to shove it or kiss their ass, nor am I saying you need to subvert your will to the company or be a free spirit within it. You've got to make those calls. You do you, based on what is ethical and aligns with your values.

Here's what I am saying: your job doesn't care about you.

You could work for a Fortune 500 company, a sprawling international corporation, a government agency, or in a twenty-person storefront. Maybe your organization was named Best Place to Work for the eighth year in a row by the Regional Alliance of Yadda Professionals. Doesn't matter.

Whatever industry and whatever perks they offer, at the end of the day, your job doesn't care about you. Brands don't want what is best for you. Neither, really, does your boss. I mean, your boss might be a mensch, but their job is not to look out for your best interests—it's to look out for the organization's.

Hardworking, talented guys sometimes forget the truth in what I'm saying. They want to be responsible. They don't want to be quitters. They want to be considered loyal and dependable. Five years down the line, they go to work the day after their child is born . . . just for a couple of hours. Ten years in, they don't consider another career-boosting offer or their spouse's wishes because "no one can manage the system I've set up." Fifteen years later, they're going through the motions instead of having the integrity to step aside for somebody who is interested in doing the job better—and in the process they're cheating themselves out of the chance to do the same thing somewhere else.

And what do they have to show for it? Maybe some bitterness and strained family relationships, and definitely lost opportunities for professional fulfillment and personal growth. All because you thought you had to prioritize the place that has their logo on your paychecks.

Your job doesn't care about you.

It's true! The company's leaders may say they do, but they care about a smooth-functioning system more, because if the system works, they don't have to spend time improving it. They care about you until you no longer fit their needs or you push back about some issue. In prosperous times, pay raises rise slowly. In dark times, they lay off people or institute furloughs. You may have been the golden child at some point, and when they see potential, they'll squeeze every ounce of ambition they can get out of you until, one way or the other, you're done.

The company moves on. The company always moves on.

You're like the puppy that no longer gets petted. Does anybody even get a freakin' gold watch anymore?

I'm not here to start a revolution. Surely this is not news to you. But in the daily grind of performance reviews, delinquent accounts, and making sure you've got income, men need to learn to do their work to the best of their abilities while also putting themselves and their family first.

Get all you can out of your company. It's not selfish. They're sure as shit trying to get everything they can out of you. I'm not talking about stealing staplers or lying on your time sheets. There's no honor in that. I mean work hard, do the best you can, and be someone your team can count on. But also ask for what you want—a promotion, a raise, a new title, a stake in the company, a seat at the table on a major account, a professional development opportunity . . . above all, a chance to have your voice heard. Set boundaries about after-hours and weekend work. Do freelance projects if you want, as long as it isn't a conflict of interest with your regular job and you aren't doing it on company time.

Not every company job in corporate America is a dismal experience, but too many of them turn promising careers into grunt-work jobs for many men. They want hamsters on the wheel, not creative, productive members of a strong team. They tell you where the carrot is and then keep moving it farther away. Many companies don't want you enjoying your residual income. They want you clawing to make higher sales goals each quarter and feeling guilty if you don't hit their numbers. It's a total mind-fuck and a quality-of-life killer.

I worked at Insgroup, and I did damn good work for them. But the partners and board and shareholders had priorities that had nothing to do with me. That's fine. My bosses knew my life didn't end when the workday did. They supported my podcasting and executive decathlete competitions, and I was transparent about why those nonwork ventures were important to me and sustained my personal health. It was a partnership that worked well for me, and I held my head high when I represented them and succeeded in my work goals.

But you know what: I hold my head high when I represent me, myself, and I, too. And I'll always care about my family above my career.

Make sure you do too.

Socrates and Change

"The secret of change is to focus all of your energy not on fighting the old, but on building the new."

Socrates said this. Even in ancient Greece, I guess grudges and stubbornness were a thing.

Change doesn't follow; it leads. If you can embrace differences, engage in healthy debate, and maintain strength of conviction, then disagreement can be respected. You have a choice to be tolerant and understanding or rigid and confrontational.

Some days that choice is harder than others . . . but it's still a choice.

CHAPTER 18

Practice What You Preach

Take control of your life, with integrity
and responsibility.

*There's an adage. They say you never start a company to set it
up for acquisition. You never start a company to sell it. That's
a mistake, because then you'll never sell it. I've thought about
this, because I've established a lot of relationships and friendships in the industry with other commercial bakery owners.
I've got a friend of mine who owns this massive bakery in a two-
hundred-thousand-square-foot facility, and he's been offered
$100 million and $120 million, respectively, on a 10X and
12X multiplier because he's killing it doing national work.
And he won't sell it.*

I said, "Are you out of your effin' mind?! It's $100 million!"

*He said, "Look, this is my baby. You've got a wife and
kids. You'd probably sell it in a heartbeat so you can retire
and be done and spend time with your family."*

I said, "Yeah, of course."

He said, "I don't know if I could allow someone else to come in and watch them make mistakes and me not be able to control any of that."

I said, "What if you could just stay on and negotiate that into the deal?"

So I started thinking about it. What if we're fortunate enough to build this and be able to attract a buyer? Look, if you set your company up for acquisition, you've basically pissed off the right people. Here's a company that's either taking up more space on the shelf next to us at the grocery store or has taken a market share from us in this specific vertical that we should be penetrating more. Fuck 'em. Let's just buy 'em. Right? That happens in our industry just as it does anywhere else. So I always joke, how much do I want to piss 'em off though to the extent that they're like, "We're going to acquire the brand. We've got the production or the capacity, the operations and the distribution to just take this in house. Thank you, here's your payday."

I don't know if I'd like that entirely.

— **TASOS KATSAOUNIS,** founder and CEO, the Bread Man Baking Company, on *The Midlife Male* podcast, Episode #128

* * *

While the Bread Man keeps baking amazing food and surely raising the valuation of his business (regardless of whether he ever decides to sell), his musings got very real for me when the insurance company I'd been at for fifteen years was acquired.

Nine months later, I was gone. I can't say it was the smoothest corporate exit in history—or even in my own work history (though I've certainly had worse).

Previous Job: Shareholder at Insgroup; Advisor, Insgroup/ BRP.

Current Job: Helping Men Maximize Middle Age.

It's not as though it was unexpected. The writing was on the wall when we were acquired. As a shareholder this was fantastic news. It became obvious to me that while this was a new beginning for my partners, it was the beginning of the end there for me and an opportunity to set in motion what I really want to do at this stage of my life.

Still, it's a shock. The fear of the unknown and navigating a new financial reality always is. But I didn't panic. More than anything, I felt a weight being lifted. The funny thing is I didn't even know how stressed I was until I wasn't holding onto it anymore.

I don't care about anybody else's opinions on the matter. You know what they say about opinions and assholes: everybody's got one. I want my family and me to be happy. Being with my wife makes me happy. Being a dad makes me happy. Helping people makes me happy. Training makes me happy. Telling great stories makes me happy.

I asked myself, "What are your five-to-ten-year career goals? What are your lifestyle goals? What are your ultimate life goals?"

None of them included insurance. At this point in my life, my lifestyle goals are as important as my professional goals.

The beauty of the transition is that it provides a rocket booster to the Midlife Male Movement that I've been all in on since my early forties.

That's the great thing: I'm old enough that, probably like a lot of you, I've had numerous careers. I'm stoked about the next stage of my life—in large part because more than ever I see how my work and personal lives are set up to be aligned.

That's the practice-what-you-preach part. My current job is certainly not new. You know my mission to help men maximize middle age has been fundamental to who I am for a long time. I've been saying for years now on the pod, on social media, and in my newsletter that you don't follow your passion without a foundation that sets you up to pursue it responsibly and successfully.

Equity in our house is solid. College is set up for our boys. Cars are paid off. We don't live extravagantly. Kate and I have talked about this for months. We knew the day would come. It did, and we're prepared.

I've said I'm not driven by money, but I want enough of it to ensure the freedom to live the lifestyle I choose. You give some guys $100 million and they say, "Great! I'm only $900 million away from a billion." Some of us have different goals and numbers. And you may still need to do a lot of calculations and conversations to determine what you want to get out of an exit strategy or a buyout. These are problems of prosperity, and if you're fortunate enough to be in that position, take into account all the important factors:

- What does my family need? What do they want?
- Did we meet the goals we set out when we started?

- Does my organization still give me purpose and enjoyment?
- Do I want fuck-you money?
- Is the bird in the hand worth two in the bush?
- If I don't grab the bird in the hand, will I regret it later?

Whatever position you're in, if you're considering making a change, be sure that you can.

Survey your situation. If you're not sure what you can do, make sure that you are talking to people that can help advise you through that. These are not decisions and choices that you can make lightly and without proper preparation. You cannot be irresponsible if you've got people that count on you and depend on you financially, emotionally, and physically.

None of us know the future, but I can confidently say to you I'm practicing what I preach. With the data I have and the planning I've done, I'm doing right by myself and my family. Life is finite. Time is the only resource We can't make more of it, so we've got to make the most of it.

This shift in my world opened the door for me to elevate the Midlife Male Movement big time, including the publication of this book. After taking care to ensure a smooth transition for my former colleagues and clients in my previous career, the chains were off!

I'm set now to turn what started out as a personal passion into the premier digital media platform for middle-aged men seeking to maximize their lives and the brands who want to reach them. I have amazing brand partners, a performance-coaching business, and a thriving podcast and newsletter.

I owe it to these guys to give them everything I've got. The experience I've gained over the past fifteen years helps me to be a better coach for my clients going through similar emotions and experiences. My time and my focus are to make sure that I overdeliver on the investment they've made in me and help these men to achieve their goals.

Midlife Males are the fastest-growing consumer-products demographic in the world. I'm thrilled to be working with the brands that want to reach them so that together we can provide them with options, recommendations, and advice from the very best in leadership and quality.

What's my legacy going to be? Where can I make the most impact?

It's not going to be dying at a desk making somebody else rich. If I can help as many men as possible to repurpose, refocus, and recommit to being the best father, husband, and leader they can be, then that's enough. I'm chasing total life wellness, not what's young and trendy.

I'm not afraid of aging. I'm afraid of staying in the same place, losing my curiosity, and not taking the best care of myself and my family mentally, physically, and financially as I can.

This is a movement based on helping, which is where I've always felt most at home. My mission is simple: to redefine how midlife is currently looked at as a crisis. The middle is the sweet spot. We have the opportunity and experience to make the next phase our best phase.

I'm headed there, and I invite you to continue on the journey along with me.

Get Moving

Answer the door

There are a lot of Midlife Males who go it alone or find excuses to keep doing what they've always done, even when the Universe is knocking down the front door to send them a clear message that their way is not working.

Which one(s) are you? And what changes are you going to make so that you open the next knock on your door ready to listen and get better results?

- Mr. Dodged a Bullet. My heart attack? That was a one-time deal. I'm good now. Get me the half-pound burger and a shake before the game starts.

- Mr. Not Right Now. As in, I know I need to make changes, and I will, but *not right now*. I just gotta get a few things figured out. Then I'll take care of my finances, weight, family . . . yadda yadda yadda.

- Mr. Mighty Mouse. Here I come to save the day! I've got to get back to the office right now because everything will fall apart without me. Everyone else is incompetent and lazy.

- Mr. Mansplainer. Can you stop talking now so I can listen to myself think? If I need to learn something, I'll be sure to let myself know.

- Mr. Refuse to Chill. I've got to take my family on this expensive vacation that I won't enjoy because I feel like shit, look like shit, and am in complete denial.

There are better options:

- Mr. Almost There. I know my life looks good on paper, but I've got some tweaking to do for authentic contentment and fulfillment.

- Mr. Overindexed. I'm all in on one or two areas of life, but the other Fs are suffering.

When opportunity knocks, will you be here?

- Mr. Midlife Male. I'm dialed in. I have a coach. I'm self-aware and in touch with what I want and need. I'm going to keep doing me, bro. It's working, but it's also always a work in progress.

Getting Real on Risk

Downer alert: people die.

If you're in your forties and fifties, you'll notice that more people die. And it's not just the aunts and uncles anymore, but high school and college classmates coming across the social media feeds.

I know a guy in a mountain biking group who had a fatal accident on a group ride. His family was devastated, and he didn't have his estate in order, leaving them in an even worse place and causing his friends to set up a Go-FundMe site for them.

I know a guy who was working himself to death. He had to get resuscitated by the EMTs in front of his family at the swimming pool. He survived. Will he make changes?

Insurance, risk management, worst-case scenarios. These are not fun topics. I'll break it down for you, though, because this shit is as real as it gets.

These things don't happen until they do. If you don't take care of life until you're desperate for money, in jail, or with a terminal illness, you've created problems for yourself and your loved ones.

Get yourself a trusted insurance advisor, attorney, financial planner, and doctor.

When you do:

☐ every doctor's visit isn't stressful.

☐ a buy-sell agreement with your partner or a prenup with your spouse aren't triggers for dissent but just rationale negotiations when the heat is not turned up.

☐ you remove the likelihood of the word *crisis*. Preparation provides peace of mind. We're searching for better quality of life, and this helps create it.

Pro tips: You want to set up your next generation to be rich? Then buy life insurance young, lots of it. Disability insurance is another thing. That shit will bankrupt you fast. That's the worst of all possible worlds.

The Fourth F
FOOD

- [ ] What food energizes you?
- [ ] What do you do when you have a drink?
- [ ] Do you eat what you want or what's put in front of you?
- [ ] What would be your "last supper"?
- [ ] When was your last personalized nutritional analysis?

CHAPTER 19

Will You Pay Your Farmer
or Your Doctor?

You are responsible for your health.

I had been working as a professional chef for fifteen years, and I was well established in my career, but I was living with an autoimmune disease, rheumatoid arthritis. I was on tons of pills a day and weekly infusion, daily injections. I was overweight and could barely get out of bed in the morning. My career was doing really well, but my body was suffering the consequences.

It got to the point where I had been in and out of the hospital every couple of months, and I had a really severe health crisis. I developed bacterial meningitis, an infection in my brain, and I basically died in the ICU. When I was able to come back from that, I had one of those classic near-death experiences where you see the light and you see the other side and made a conscious choice in that state of unconsciousness to come back. When I came back, I made a commitment to myself that I was going to make significant changes to how I was living my life, because if I didn't, I wasn't going to be around.

The first thing I did, which I think was fundamentally the most important thing, was to stop thinking of myself as a victim. It took a lot for me to put on my big-boy pants and say, "Fuck this. Maybe this is not my fault that I'm here, but some of it is my responsibility, and regardless of what got me to this place of being a completely sick person, I need to take ownership over my own well-being." It's important to me to recognize that there is a difference between being sick and having a sickness. I was really mired in this idea that I was a sick person, which meant that anything I went through was not my fault and the result of outside forces.

Once I was able to get past that and start to recognize that I'm a strong human being, that I have means, I have will, I have drive, I have discipline, but I also happen to be living with a sickness, it was hugely empowering. For one, it meant I wasn't at the mercy of the medical community. And two, that I could do a lot on my own to affect change and have autonomy over my health. The hard part is that the hospitality industry is one that is really good at taking care of other people but we're pretty shitty at taking care of ourselves.

Anytime somebody is going through a crisis like this, particularly a health crisis, it is unreasonable to expect that person to be able to just Horatio Alger themselves up and get on with just, "Hey, get over yourself." It takes a community. I was very lucky that I had the support of my family, my team, my friends. Everyone rallied around me to help me make changes.

We talk about illness as being contagious, but I think health is just as contagious. When you start to make good decisions about your health and your own well-being, it starts to rub off on the people around you, and they make better decisions. It begets a community of solidarity and accountability.

It's very costly to invest in your own health. Making the decision to buy better-quality ingredients for myself, that's expensive. I'm going to invest in acupuncture, which is not covered by insurance. I'm going to invest in a yoga practice. All of these things add up and cost money, so there's that financial aspect. Then, what if my businesses are thriving but at the expense of my health? Is that really worth it at the end of the day? Is it worth it for me to kill myself for extra dollars, or is it better to forego and say no, which is something that was really difficult for me to do? It still is difficult for me to do. I'm trying to get better at it, learning that I can't do every project. There are lots of opportunities that could have financial upside, but there is going to be an opportunity cost in doing them that plays out in my well-being and my health.

I was at the farmer's market having a conversation with one of the farmers that I buy produce from, and she said something really profound that resonated with me. She said, "You can either pay your farmer today, or you can pay your doctor tomorrow."

And what's the real value if you say yes and you do a half-baked job of it, or you're exhausted, or you fucked up your schedule and you should be doing something else because there's too many things going on? It's important to, as best you can, prioritize the things that are really of value to you. And oftentimes, I've found, the things that are the highest value are not necessarily financially valuable. They're experi-

entially valuable. They're more about greater fulfillment that is beyond the financial.

I've never thought of health as a destination: Now I've got health! Box checked. Like a high-performance sports car, you have to maintain it. If you don't, it's going to go to shit. Having gone through this transition, I have a story to share. I have an important message. I have a greater meaning in my life. It's not just to cook delicious food so people can say, "Oh, that was really great." Rather, it's to help people understand the capacity they have to care for themselves with the choices they make on a daily basis. It doesn't mean I'm going to give you all the answers, because I don't have all the answers. I'm just as fucked up as everybody else. I know some things that work for me and have been able to do some things that from the outside might seem completely unrealistic. But I'm not remarkable. I'm just like everybody else. Yes, I was able to reverse what is considered an incurable autoimmune disease. I lost sixty-five pounds. But I'm not unusual. Most people can do this, with enough discipline and support and guidance.

— **SEAMUS MULLEN,** award-winning New York chef, restaurateur, and cookbook author, on *The Midlife Male* podcast, Episode #58

* * *

We talk about "the turnaround" or "the comeback" all the time in business and in sports. We praise the corporate CEOs and quarterbacks who supposedly engineer these massive changes that alter the fortunes for their organizations. But for me, far more impressive is when individuals reverse a downward spiral in their personal health. Having a support system can make it much more possible to enact that change.

You may not be doing it entirely on your own, but ultimately *you* are the one who is in the arena. *You* choose whether to eat processed food with a half-life into the next century. *You* choose whether to do an elimination diet to determine what you're putting into your body that is killing you. *You* determine if you make good choices for a day, a week, or over many years. My hat is off to the people who realize their obesity, their smoking, their drinking, or their diet is simply not acceptable anymore.

Your nutritional choices have to be at the heart of this change because other than sleep, it's the only aspect of your health you are guaranteed to confront daily. You may or may not exercise, socialize, pray, meditate, work, or play, but you are going to ingest something—or choose to fast—every single day.

I say often that I don't have "it" figured out, so I want to keep learning and growing. This is more relevant to your food choices than you might realize. People search for just the right diet or the right "take" on what you should or shouldn't do when it comes to eating healthy. Sadly, what often happens is paralysis by analysis. Instead of taking small steps to enact change, people want to swallow every bit of information they can so they don't make the wrong call.

Change your mind

The reality is you need to make decisions based on what works for you, and that comes from being more attuned to your body and its reactions to what you put in it. This is not a one-size-fits-all situation. And you know what? You can change your mind. You're a big boy. If people bust on you for not being consistent, maybe they're the ones who need to look at the life they are living.

For me, my stance on the Paleo diet has changed. When I was hard core into CrossFit, I went full caveman for a while. I know plenty of people who swear by it, and I'm not trying to change their minds. It doesn't work for me now, and that's all that matters. I change my mind based on conversations with experts (a prime reason why I enjoy my weekly podcast guests), my own research, my own experiences, and my own needs and goals going forward. I'm not going to eat something because a twenty-year-old influencer told me to or because my mom says that's how we do it. I'll give her more of a platform to express her views than just about anybody else, but it's my life. No one knows my body better than me.

If you're not willing to change your opinions, you're in decay. That's the hard truth that stubborn people don't want to admit. They think rigid adherence to how they've always done things is a show of strength. The real show of strength is recognizing the problem and seeking out solutions that will solve it.

Take small steps

You know the old saying about when the right time to plant a tree is, right?

Twenty years ago.

When's the next best time?

Right now.

Maybe you've spent twenty years allowing your body to decline. That doesn't mean you can't begin to turn things around right now. My guess is you had reasons why you let that happen. Maybe you felt you had to compromise on your eating habits while you built your company. You didn't have time to eat well. Maybe your ex-wife did the cooking and you fell into line with her food choices. I'm not here to judge whether that was reality or a story you told yourself. I really don't care.

The only question that matters now is what you will do for yourself . . . now. Yes, now. As in today now.

Get Moving

Will you take control of your nutrition?

- Will you lower your soda intake?
- Will you cut back your refined sugars?
- Will you schedule an appointment with your doctor or a nutritionist to develop a plan customized for you?
- Will you ask the people closest to you how your health affects them?
- Will you prioritize eating meals with your loved ones on a regular basis?

Rather than commiserate over all the things we can't do, why not focus on what we can? Here are six things I'm doing to be better that I have 100 percent control over.

1. **Sleeping more.** I'm getting to bed earlier, improving the quality of rest, and still waking up at 6:00 a.m.

2. **Walking.** Some days it's just a couple miles and some coffee; others it's mountain bike trails with a forty-pound vest.

3. **Eating better.** The quality of my meals has improved tremendously as I'm eating at home more, using fresh ingredients, and trying new recipes. When we take out, I'm ordering healthier, as I'm not as "influenced" by all the other meals passing by my table at the restaurant.

4. **Serving.** Being of service, communicating, and showing empathy, at work and in all areas of my life, provide purpose and connection.

5. **Creating.** Whether it's the podcast I'm recording, the Instagrams I'm posting, this book I'm writing, the music I'm playing, new exercises I'm trying, or "domestic" skills I'm picking up, I'm creatively inspired each day.

6. **Developing new opportunities.** I'm investing in people, brands, and collaborations that are growth-mindset-driven, have scale, and combine personal passion with professional expertise.

CHAPTER 20

Diet Is a Four-Letter Word

Nutrition is not one size fits all.
Do your homework, and listen to the pros.

The nutrition aspect of what I was learning in my independent studies at school was extraordinary. I was able to apply that to sport. And then after I finished wrestling, I just didn't want to get fat again. I literally saw a picture of this guy named Boyer Coe on the cover of Iron Man *magazine, lookin' like big huge arms. I'm like, "Oh my God, that guy gets laid. That's crazy. I want to look like that. He's not fat." That's what I wanted to dive into and learn about, so I could create a physique that I wouldn't be fat or bullied. So it came from a place of insecurity but a real desire to learn about the science of this. And I applied it. I tried it, and that didn't work. And I tried it, and that didn't work. And then discovering how lipid profile management—the information about your HDLs and LDLs and triglyceride levels and your glucose and this thing called HBA1C, which is a diabetic marker—really plays into how you should be eating. That's how I got into this whole sports nutrition and metabolic science.*

I've had so many calls about plant-based protocol, which is great, assuming you can manage sugars well. In the world of lipid-profile assessment, though, like me, I've got a high HBA1C, even when I'm on foods. I don't use sugars well. My triglyceride levels will elevate easily with a sugar consumption. I crave sugars. If there was cookie dough on your shoulder, I'd eat your arm to get it. I swear to God, I would. Why would I start a plant-based food protocol? That's a bad idea for me because it's primarily sugar. Me? I'm more a fat-and-protein guy. Lots of fatty fish, a bunch of eggs, a bunch of nuts.

If you don't know what kind of guy you are, usually that question hits when you are in that middle-aged place. Right? You've made it in your career path. You're not worried about your car payment anymore. You've got some money. You've sacrificed a bunch of health to work your ass off. Now you're a little upside down in your waistline and you're like, "Fuck, what do I do? How do I manage this? Here I am, middle-aged. Goddammit, my pants don't fit and I feel like crap and my energy level's low." That's the biggest thing I hear. I see between twenty-six and thirty-four people a day roll through this place. When I first meet them, it's always, "My energy sucks." It's not even so much about their waistline. It's about "my energy pattern blows." Eating is so important to create a consistent energy pattern. Most folks have an adversarial relationship with their scale weight, and they end up with an adversarial relationship with their food. They view food as a mechanism that promotes fat gain and weight gain.

So here's something to think about: here's that guy and he's 250 or 280, whatever. He's having trouble with his waist-line, so he stops eating and it gets worse. If undereating worked, people wouldn't be fat. It's easy to skip a meal. It's very hard to eat your meals. In that place, especially in Guy World, if you start to undereat, you really start to suppress testosterone levels too, which will adversely affect libido and even cause more hoarding of fat, so it's always foods first.

In Guy World, you say, What can I do immediately? You get rid of anything inflammatory because those things are aging, so no yeast, no mold, no dairy, no gluten. And no beans—beans are high mold. That's easy. It just means no breads, no muffins—if it sits in a bag and is placed on a shelf, you can't have it. So you focus on one-ingredient starch-es—potatoes, yams, oatmeal, oat flakes, oat puffs. Those are your buddies. Look at your starches and say to [them], "How many ingredients are in you?" If they tell you more than one, don't have it. OK, cool, but now you say, "Don't I need pro-tein? I'm exercising."

Exercise is interesting. You're in that middle-aged place and you joined a gym, but you still view food as adversarial. You've got a strategy for your training but not for your kitch-en or your bedroom, like your sleep patterns and sleep hy-giene. You're wicked sore, so all of a sudden you bend down to pet your cat and your back goes out. Training doesn't change physique. Training just breaks down muscle tissue, and it in-flames you. That's the job of training. It's a catabolic event. Your anabolic event, where your physique and performance change, is kitchen and bedroom—calories, heat patterns. Calories are heat energy units. Your metabolism ultimately is a function of that heat. Fat is a lipid; it's an oil or like butter.

*ill only convert to energy in a calorically hot environ-
..... Don't eat enough heat, can't burn fat. When you're
training, you want to repair your muscle tissues.*

*Overall, calories are important. Caloric consumption and
as well your protein pattern. But people confuse beans, le-
gumes, and tofu for proteins, but here's the new news—well,
it's not new news; it's old news—protein is meat with eyes,
dammit. Chicken, fish, steak, turkey, eggs. Nuts and seeds are
a separate category because it's mostly fat, little protein. But
if it can run, swim, or take a dump in the woods and has a
heartbeat, it's a protein. Everything else is freakin' sugar first.
And there might be amino acids in there if you combine them,
but it's still a sugar first. That's important to understand.
Be strategic trying to figure out your foods as a middle-aged
guy. The best time to repair muscle tissue is when your body's
at rest. Because rest time is sleep, my biggest protein meal
should be dinner. Do I need that starch at night? Do I need
rice, potato, yam at night? That's an energy-source food. It's
a sugar. You're not going to run a marathon after dinner, for
Chrissake. So protein and veggies, dinner. Have your starch
at lunch when you need that energy pattern. And then always
after dinner, a little fruit, a little sugar, to spike your insulin
and promote a deep sleep. Food programming is strategic. Do
not undereat.*

> — **PHIL GOGLIA,** founder of PFC Nutrition, partner at
> Split Nutrition, and author of *Turn Up the Heat:
> Unlock the Fat-Burning Power of Your Metabolism*, on
> *The Midlife Male podcast*, Episode #101

* * *

The four-letter word I really hate is *diet*. People get overly zealous, flustered, or exhausted trying to eat "correctly," as though you can eat correctly any more than you can have sex correctly or be a friend correctly or parent correctly. There are many paths you can take to get the results you want in life in the areas that matter most.

Keto. Paleo. Intermittent fasting. How do you choose? You're busy. You want somebody to give you a confident answer so you can just plug and play what you're going to put into your body. Right there is the problem though. If some influencer or diet-book author sounds like they know what they're talking about, people hop on board because the person either made it sound easy or sounded firm in how certain they were it would work.

The more I've discovered in talking to experts—certified nutritionists, strength-training coaches, personal trainers, chefs, healthy-food entrepreneurs—the more I've come to accept ambiguity with my food and supplement choices. That doesn't mean I give myself license to slack off or that I've decided it's a futile quest or not important. It just means that my nutritional choices deserve the same level of self-grace and allowance for mistakes as every other area of my life.

Food and nutrition are a lifestyle. Unless you're competing to win Mr. Olympia, or have some health problem that is prohibiting you from regular eating, then you should be focused on lifestyle choices, not a rigid diet. And in case I haven't been clear up to this point, perfection does not exist in life—not for people who went to school to know this stuff, and sure as hell not for the rest of us who turn to the smartest of them to get schooled about it.

Here are a few tips for you to consider as you're figuring out what works for you:

- Simple works. Like quality brands and high-level physical activity exercises, the fundamentals and basics still work. One-ingredient foods should be your priority. You don't have to go on a designer diet to find a magic bullet for weight loss or muscle gain or to unclog your arteries.

- Start with a visit to the doctor. If you haven't been on a food program before, you probably aren't going to know what you need. You may not even be entirely clear on what you want. So go see your doctor or a certified nutritionist. Get your blood work done. Give yourself and your experts something to work with when they start asking you questions that will help ensure they're giving you the best advice to create a successful foundation. You can go broke trying to change your nutritional habits just find out you're doing it all wrong. This is a solid up-front investment in your health.

- Listen to professionals. Related to the above point, influencers aren't experts. You have to take ownership of the goal setting, research, and planning to get results that work for you. If you don't understand what you're reading or being told, ask questions. Don't do something just because somebody with twenty thousand followers told you to, unless that somebody is a credentialed professional. I wouldn't even assume the manufacturer has my best interests at heart. I'm not saying some of them don't, but I'm doing my research before I decide they do. Corporations have massive marketing and publicity budgets to tell you what they want you to hear. If somebody is trying to sell me cases of something, I check it out. It's no different than a stylist, a trainer, a financial advisor, a life coach, or anybody else in position to assert authority over you—do your homework.

- Extremes aren't the answer. If you're told you need to eat bacon all day in one program or salad all day in another, maybe you're not working with someone who knows anything about creating a program that is sustainable. That's just not how this works. If you get hit by a bus and are pissed off because you haven't eaten a cheeseburger in four years, that's a shitty way to leave this mortal coil. Bottom line: if you deprive yourself too much, that's not sustainable.

- Don't beat yourself up when you don't get immediate results. Actually, don't be fooled if you lose weight on a diet plan in the first few weeks and think you've found the answer. If you haven't been following any plan and then are following a plan, you likely *will* see weight loss. But again, is it sustainable? Are you creating, or at least not addressing, other problems by focusing solely on weight loss? Have you and your medical professional taken into account your family history? Because that may require some adaptations. All food programming is imperfect and so are you, but stay focused. Even doing 75 percent of an expert's plan is going to lead to sustainable gains.

- Just because it's simple doesn't mean it's easy. This is a new *learned* responsibility. Understanding and applying nutritional information is no different than exercising a muscle you haven't used before. It's probably a weak muscle until you start training it. You're creating new habits for yourself. Use apps that help keep you accountable and remind you. Find foods and products that make it convenient for you to follow through on your plan—this is where understanding your goals and doing your research is important, because convenience for convenience's sake is not what you want; convenience to help you sustain your plan is. Reading labels and understanding them will become second nature, but not right away. Experts and friends who know what you're going through will have supportive words and hacks that keep you on track.

One time I just happened to be eating breakfast at the same restaurant as Arnold Schwarzenegger. I'm interested in what fit people do and eat to stay in shape, so I've got one eye on my business associate, who I'm trying to have a conversation with, and the other eye on what the Terminator is eating this morning. It looked like oatmeal and fruit—and as far as I could see, he didn't put brown sugar on it.

I'm not telling you to be a protein-and-fat guy like Phil, or eat Arnold's breakfast of champions, or spend fifty dollars a month on amino acids or any other supplement. I'm saying your job is to find what works for you, through trial and error and lots of questions. When you get it right—or some semblance of right—you're going to find yourself in a better place.

Gratitude and Attitude

You are the sum of the five people you spend the most time with.

That could not be any clearer.

Play up.

Don't settle.

Do whatever it takes to surround yourself with mentors, advisors, investors, thinkers, people who are smarter, fitter, funnier, wealthier, healthier . . .

You'll learn, grow, expand your mind and network, and begin to see things through a different lens.

Be interested, and be interesting.

If you're relevant—personally, professionally, or even if you're just fun—you'll be invited to stick around.

CHAPTER 21
Excel with Quality Ingredients

Emphasize quality. Embrace competition.
You'll like the results.

We want to give you only what you need. And there's a big difference between needing something and wanting something. I saw this firsthand when I had to cut out dairy. Our goal is to be there for the people that truly need us and the people who can't have or don't want dairy, gluten, soy, eggs, nuts, or meat.

I love competition in the space as long as it's good. My biggest fear is more entrants that come into the space with a product that doesn't taste good. Because then people may never come back to the category. But the more people that come into plant-based with products that are good, I think it's great for us. A rising tide's going to lift all the boats, and then ultimately once a customer comes into the category, it's up to them to decide: I like the category. I've shopped the category. What brand resonates with me? What do I like? What ingredients do I like? What brand is doing what I want? Who's drinking it? What people are involved with it? What are people saying about it?

Let the consumer make the decision. What I don't want is some competitor with a product that's inferior and then no one's going to try us. Good-tasting competition is a benefit to all of us.

— **JEFF MROZ,** former NFL quarterback and cofounder of OWYN, on *The Midlife Male* podcast, Episode #78

* * *

I've talked to plenty of chefs, restauranteurs, food and supplement producers, and clean-food advocates. It's not a space for the faint of heart. Margins are slim. Definitions are slippery. To both retain your integrity and turn a profit is a balancing act.

But really, couldn't I make the same statement about any industry? Any space we spend time in? Competition is everywhere. Truly differentiating yourself on factors that matter—quality, service, speed, innovation—is what matters. Many in our society what to show they are independent or unique by just being outrageous or stupid. It works for some for a while, but it doesn't last.

You're at the stage of your life where you need to choose quality over quantity. As much noise and clutter as there is in any space, you really have to do your homework on what you are going to purchase—starting with if and why you even need it—and focus on brands and people that deliver value. There's way too much smoke and mirrors, style over substance, out there. Don't choose the marketing over the content. If the product is solid, the marketing writes itself.

That's why I like Jeff's take on having more brands come into the food and beverage industry and try to take his margin share. Jeff is no dummy. He's a Yale grad. NFL coaching legend Bill Parcells handwrote a letter of reference on Jeff's behalf to Penn's Wharton School of Business to support his quarterback's application for the MBA program there—let that sink in for a minute!

Jeff is basically saying, "Bring it on!" But he's also doing something even better: he's betting on himself. And he's pursuing excellence.

You should do no less. When you find products that work for you, like OWYN, which gives you Only What You Need (see what Jeff and his cofounders did there?), you choose to celebrate and support quality brands founded by quality people.

Then the value proposition is an investment, not an expense. Investments pay you back; they give you a return. Expenses just drain your wallet with food, supplements, products, and people you don't need.

He and others in his space have a challenge: he has to decide whether to emphasize his product being plant based at the risk of getting pigeonholed or go wide and lose OWYN's distinct identity and origins.

It's a constant tension, and he doesn't claim to have all the answers. Neither do I. We figure it out as we go.

What I can tell you is to trust yourself. Trust your brand. Be aware of what you put into your body. Expect positive results in everything you do, and accept challengers. Competition creates collegiality, community. It's energetic and leads to innovation.

I hope it goes without saying, but I'm not just talking food here.

Whether you're a businessman or a consumer, make sure you bet on yourself and take part in something excellent.

I Am Not Uncertain

I am not particularly skilled at anything, nor particularly educated.

I'm capable, smart enough, and can talk to anyone and hold up my end of a conversation.

I am far more of a generalist than a specialist, so I guess you could say I'm a jack of all trades, master of none.

I'm inherently curious and believe that someone else usually has a better answer or solution to a problem than I do, so I should just ask them. Despite all of this, I'm rarely uncertain, and I make my feelings known.

I've struggled with how much to put in to areas where things haven't come easy. Should I spend more time on addressing weaknesses or strengthening strengths?

I have bounced around in a variety of professional endeavors. Some good, some not so good, some great, and some . . . let's just not talk about it.

I've had relationships that have gotten stronger personally and professionally when we've lost money in a deal and friendships that have fallen apart despite us making a profit together.

I have been fat. I have been fit.

I have been drunk. I have been sober.

I have had long luxurious hair, and I am now bald as a cue ball.

If I can somehow navigate through the ridiculousness of life, put food on the table, remain married, not screw up my kids too badly, have a few dollars in the bank, and be in pretty good shape, then any one of you guys can. I truly believe that.

And yes, I have had some advantages growing up, no doubt. I have also had some considerable disadvantages. I am not taking credit for overcoming disadvantages, and I am not accepting criticism for being born with certain advantages. It is what it is.

So what's the takeaway?

The takeaway is that at any age, at any stage, and at any time, you can make changes.

You just have to start.

You can do better, you can improve, you can figure it out.

You can start by taking a look at the man in the mirror and liking the person looking back.

For some of us, we're blessed with the ability to develop early, know exactly what we want to do, and put all the pieces of life together seamlessly. I can't imagine that's too many of us though. For those like me, we may never totally figure it out. But we still have to live. The show must always go on. It would be galactically irresponsible to give up, quit, stop, complain, or blame.

Get up, get dressed, get going.

The Fifth F
FASHION

- Are you a yellow Lamborghini guy or a classic Range Rover guy?

- What would you wear if you could wear anything?

- Do you wear a wristwatch? What kind?

- What clothing or style makes you feel confident?

- What colors are "you"?

- Do you even think of or consider fashion and style in your life?

- If you could be a spokesperson for any brand, which would it be?

- Do you have a personal style or "look"?

- How do you appear when standing next to your wife? Do you look aligned?

CHAPTER 22

If It's Good Enough for Clooney or Kanye, It's Good Enough for You

You can become a stylish MLM with just these few basic suggestions.

If you were to ask Nick Young, a.k.a. Swaggy P, he's going to definitely tell you I have a look. And he's called me out on it numerous times. I do have what I like to consider a uniform in the sense that I think it gives a little bit of a good crossover, like I look professional but I'm also not a buttoned-up-in-a-suit kind of guy. It's about finding a balance. I might have some nice chinos or dress pants and then get a little bit more casual up top, maybe a nice cardigan. I'm also lucky to have a wife who went to fashion school. I lean into her a lot. I say, "Help me out here!" because I'm around the most fashionable guys. We've attended fashion shows around the world. I think I have a little bit of style, but there's a time and a place for everything, and as I'm getting older and am representing the guys, I can't be trying to look like DeAndre [Hopkins]. That doesn't work. What do they call it? The Dad Swag? You find the balance [between what is stylish and functional for a middle-aged man]. I'm getting there. I'm excited to find that phase of the Dad Swag.

I wouldn't say I look at all brands in depth and understand everything behind the brand, but just by way of being in this industry, I have to be aware of what's new, what's hot, what's coming, not just from a brand standpoint but trends. I like to see what trends are coming, for sure, and then that leans into what brands are behind those trends. If you can connect those brands to the right people, that means it's a true partnership and it's synergistic. If you look at it and say, "How the hell did that person partner there?! That doesn't make any sense!" it doesn't feel authentic, right? That's a really important part of our job as a whole and something I'm always trying to make sure is in the forefront. DeAndre is all about health and sustainability. So when we talk about Oars and Alps, he wanted to partner with them. They're all natural. We sought that partnership out. That wasn't picking up phones or anything like that. That's authentic to him, and it so happened we were able to find a partnership that worked with them.

I can name a number of them. TO loves Febreze. Literally he's making his own candles right now. We had a multiyear partnership with them. It just made so much sense because he was so excited to do it. He's just spraying the bottles everywhere, and I'm like, "That's a lot of Febreze. We don't need all that!" But that's truly important on my side where I'm trying to build these partnerships and programs together. It's about finding those things that are authentic to the guys. It's going out there and hustling up the business. But once you've figured that out, it's not just getting connected but is this the right partnership? How does it look not just from my client's side but the brand's side, and what are we doing to ensure it's a home run?

— **DOUG SANDERS,** owner of Sanders Sports and Entertainment, on *The Midlife Male* podcast, Episode #149

* * *

Sometimes I'll ask for feedback from my eighteen- and fifteen-year-old sons about a clothing choice for an evening out. I take care of my body. I've got some fashion sense. I've got followers. I can rock this younger guy's fit, right?

Right? Boys?

Hello?

All I'm saying is, if you ask for feedback, don't be upset when you get naked honesty in return. The shake of their heads told me, "Nope, Dad, not anymore." The roll of their eyes told me, "You look ridiculous."

I'm here to tell you, there's a style tipping point beyond which a Midlife Male should not push. That sounds depressing and demoralizing, but that's not what I actually mean. I'm nearly fifty, and quite frankly there are some things I can still get away with and many that I can't. But the ship hasn't sailed on looking good; in fact, just the opposite. I say your style should get better with age.

I'm a brand guy, pure and simple. I like classic brands that are elegant and timeless, whether it's an IWC watch or RAEN sunglasses or a Prada belt. But I also like to check out emerging brands, see what they stand for, and who is representing them. I geek out on this stuff. If I discover a new grain-free tortilla chip, I immediately want to know who made them, how, and whether this going to be a thing. I like connecting brands, personalities, and people.

Style equates to confidence

My approach to fashion is about quality over quantity and linking both style and substance. Style equates to confidence, which doesn't have to cost a lot of money: simple, clean, iconic, sharp. Make the effort to make it look effortless. Develop a uniform, an understanding, and an appreciation for what works for you.

You have to decide you want that though. If your gym clothes are still from college or high school, then Houston . . . we have a problem. If the rest of your wardrobe is either chasing your youth in an effort to still look cool or is so antiquated and ill-fitting that you look ten years older, don't sweat it. Maybe you were basic in your twenties, cheugy in your thirties, and now you're in your forties grasping desperately for your style. It's never too late to develop it. I'll help you get started.

Tips for nailing your personal style

Keep it simple. Simple doesn't mean boring. The best designers and best-dressed men in the world keep their personal style simple.

Fit matters. Even more so than the brand. I see lots of guys wear very expensive top brands and look terrible because the clothes don't fit them well. Find brands and items that fit your body.

Go to a tailor and get all of your measurements done. Chances are you've been wearing things way too big. More than likely when you start wearing clothing that fits you well, it's going to feel a little bit tighter. It'll take a little getting used to, but it's worth it.

After you get your measurements done, keep the tailor. I use a tailor on everything from T-shirts to pants to loungewear, jackets, everything. Tailors are a great investment. A good tailor will make any item look better on you and like you paid a lot more for it. It costs me ten to fifteen dollars to get most items tailored. One tip: wash items first before you have them tailored. A lot of times they'll shrink, and you don't want to overtailor or make something too small, tight, or short to wear.

It doesn't matter what's in, stylish, or trendy. Clean, classic, and updated basics with a great fit will always be appropriate and in style.

Try things on. See what makes you feel good. Do you like collared shirts, or do you prefer T-shirts? Do you like V-necks (and if you do, make sure they're high V-necks and not the cheesy chest-hair-baring type) or crewnecks?

Look at fit guides. Are you short? Are you tall? Are you round or thin? What does the brand recommend?

Look at magazines and websites and see how guys your age are styled and how they look. What do you relate to? Find a couple of guys whose look you like and emulate it.

Do you like color, or do you want to keep it monochromatic? If you like color, go for it. But be responsible with color, particularly as you get older. Don't mix a bunch of wild colors together.

Consider your size and shape. Paying attention to what you look like and what you want to accentuate as well as what you want to hide can play a big role in how you create your style. Just honestly assess a few pros and cons.

For example, I happen to like monochromatic, because it makes things very simple. I basically wear black, gray, brown, and navy. I stay in the darker color palette because I sweat big time and don't want to see sweat marks through my clothes. I'm on the shorter side at five nine, so I like joggers. I prefer things a little bit more fitted to make me appear longer and taller.

All the help you need in terms of looking good for your age is out there. You can find it in the pursuit, on high-end brand sites and publications such as *GQ*, *Esquire*, *Men's Journal*, and *Men's Health*. Just be observant. If George Clooney wouldn't wear it, neither should you. If Ryan Reynolds wouldn't sport it, not a good idea for you either. If Kanye is wearing it, think again.

And trust me—if your kids are really into it, that's a hard no for you. My boys can go after the fashion flavor of the moment. Meanwhile, I'll continue to work on dressing appropriately, stylishly, and as perfectly as I can for myself at middle age.

Get Iconic

The Scheinman uniform

My personal uniform is incredibly simple. For everyday, it's Rhone joggers and Element T-shirts. Rhone makes the best underwear and socks as well. I wear GREATS brand sneakers. This uniform is incredibly versatile. I can wear this out to almost any meeting. I can put a blazer over it, substitute a Reign tech hoodie, or put a vest over it. I can dress it up or dress it down.

A few other preferences and style comments of mine—not that they need to be yours, I just want to share my thought process. You can have some fun trying out new looks and giving yourself agency to determine what you like.

- I prefer crewneck T-shirts to V-necks and almost anything to a collar. So, when I'm wearing lightweight sweaters or anything, they're typically a crewneck.

- I will wear anything I can to get away from having to wear a button-down shirt. In today's world, a perfectly fitted, high-quality, crisp T-shirt with a great pair of slacks or joggers and an impeccable pair of shoes, watch, belt, and sunglasses can get you in almost anywhere.

- Just as you can't out-train a poor diet, you cannot outdress poor grooming or poor health. If you want to look your best in clothing, be in shape and be impeccably well groomed.

- I know shopping online can be overwhelming. Also, you don't know how things really fit, and there are too many choices. Start with the basics. Order a few things at a time. Use a fit guide that most quality brands have on their website, and if you know your measurements, it will help you tremendously in getting pleasing results.

- Keep the accessories to a minimum. A great watch, belt, and sunglasses will suffice.

- Looking good extends to the gym. You can and should look great when you train. I prefer shorts with the liners in them because I don't have to deal with underwear, particularly when I travel. If you want to do color in your workout clothes, keep it on the top or the bottom, but not both. Ditch the old-school high socks that go halfway or more up your calf muscle.

Greg's Style Pro/Con List

Fulfilling	Bullshit
Authenticity	Influencers
Sustainability	Fads and trends
Consistency	Quick fixes and seven-minute abs
Unapologetic	Catering and conforming
Simplicity	Complicating things
Purposeful collaborations	Small talk
Taking the dog for a walk	Being concerned the dog will track in mud
Being alone	Being a loner
Longevity	Instant Gratification
Producing	Consuming
How it feels	How it looks

CHAPTER 23

Be the Watch

Embrace the knowledge that the best part of you is below the surface.

At a pretty young age, I was exposed to watches. I collected them and saved up my pennies. Literally. I had a five-gallon jug in my closet that I filled up with pennies, nickels, dimes, whatever. It was so heavy that my parents got concerned. It was an old house, second story, and this thing was full. Five gallons of coins. And I bought a watch with it. I counted everything out. I knew exactly the watch. I calculated tax. I was a little kid when I was doing that. I've always collected watches and always been a tinkerer since a young age. It was a Freestyle Tide watch, digital obviously. It was black and orange, and I had been wanting this watch for so long. When it first came out, I got it, and I actually got serial number one. I didn't know it when I bought it, but it was serial number one on the back. I still have that watch.

I got into USC, immediately got into the Marshall School of Business there, but then quickly realized that business school isn't necessarily for the tinkerer. Now I think there's a little more exposure to entrepreneurship in college, but back then it didn't feel like anyone was making those kinds of moves. Seemed like everyone was going into some consultant positions that didn't appeal to me.

The goal behind my company is to increase awareness of mechanical watches. I noticed as I was going through school and working as a watchmaker for Audemars Piguet and Vacheron Constantin, so many people I interacted with outside of the watch world had never heard of or interacted with a mechanical watch. They just thought all watches had batteries or some sort of electronic component in them. A big goal for me was to create a watch that is not so expensive as these brands with hundreds of years of history, all of this handmade aspect that goes into it. That's all wonderful and important to watchmaking, but with modern advances we can actually keep the cost much lower so we can expose more people to mechanical watches.

I feel like buying a quartz watch right now for $500–600 is a total loss. You already have that in your iPhone and your car. We have all these electronic clocks around us, so it's not really about time. It's about everything behind the face of that watch, everything that went into it, all that history. That's all there, but it's being done in a way that it's more attainable.

I believe that slow growth of the business is important. We've made it past the five-year mark. Hopefully we'll make it past the ten-year mark. Eventually I'd love to see this business exist without me. I'd love to see a couple hundred years from now, people saying, "Was there a Weiss? Is that some-body's name? Is that why the watch is named that?"

When we're sending watches to Cupertino, when some-body from Apple buys one of our watches and has it delivered to their office, I love that feeling. A lot of times I will hear from people who say nobody's going to be wearing a watch, everybody's going to be wearing an Apple watch; that's the future. I don't really believe that. I think there's a place for both. If you're a young person that has an Apple watch and you're wearing your Apple watch all the time, what are you going to do when you go out on a date? What are you going to do when you have a big meeting or a job interview? Some-thing like that, there's no reason to have a phone on your wrist. It's almost saying the person sitting across from you is not important if your wrist is buzzing the whole time and alerts are popping up.

— **CAMERON WEISS,** founder and CEO of Weiss Watch
Company, on *The Midlife Male* podcast, Episode #95

* * *

Among his many wonderful personal traits, my dad passed down his New York Islanders fandom and his Audemars watch. He was a watch guy, and each of my brothers got one of his watches when he passed away. I was just seven-teen years old when I gained possession of it, and I'm sure I didn't fully appreciate its craftsmanship or meaning. But I'm not stupid; I knew it was special to him. I'm not a very ornate person like my dad was, but now it's my dearest possession of sentimental value as well as just being an incredible timepiece.

Sports teams get handed down generation to generation. So do watches. I'll always be a watch guy.

A watch is the male jewelry, the accoutrement, that is timeless because it is built on stories: 1) Audemars Piguet's illustrious brand and the personal histories of its founders before my dad's watch was ever crafted, 2) the making of that individual watch by Swiss technicians, and 3) my family's connection to it. Taken together, it's a three-part tale that is irreplaceable.

I bought my first Weiss watch at STAG Provisions in Austin, and I will get a second one to have the opportunity to pass each of them down to my two sons. I get more positive feedback about my Weiss than anything else I wear, and I wear it with great confidence. I've sat at the state-of-the-art workshop in Torrance, California, and seen the intricate tools used to craft it. I've spoken to Cameron and seen his patient persistence and attention to the art and science of mechanical watchmaking. I take pride in wearing something for which I know the entrepreneur and his story. I get a charge out of that. That's who I want to support.

My theory is that food tastes better when I know who made and cooked it. Clothes and accessories feel better when I know who made them. A watch is this theory fully realized.

When you look at the front side of my Weiss, it is beautiful—a classic design, manually wound, and dedicated only to the purpose of telling time.

Now turn it over. Underneath the watch face, there is so much more going on. There you see the movement of 120 pieces—some Swiss brands have nearly five hundred parts—that are traditionally hand finished and decorated. It takes inspiration from vintage gauges and aviation and incorporates them into modern design. There are no off-the-shelf parts to compose a timepiece. Each step in its development is a marvel of engineering to make it last . . . and to make a not-so-simple process exude simplicity.

The inner workings of the Weiss are only available if you look more closely, but they are there. You don't realize all that is happening beneath the surface until you do. That's when you know the watch is something special.

Does that sound like the Midlife Male? Does that sound like you?

How do you want to be remembered a couple hundred years from now? Will your sons and daughters and their children for generations to come talk about the commitment to excellence, style, and hard work that was instilled in them from a tinkerer, an entrepreneur, a gentleman? Maybe those conversations will be about decades of nostalgia or success, but wherever they stem from, would you want any less in the self-branding you put out to the world every day now?

Be the watch.

Simple and Unapologetic

Give me a simple and unapologetic style all day long. Here are a few brands (personal and product) that I identify with:

- Jesse Itzler
- Rich Roll

- Ryan Michler
- Laird Hamilton
- Tim McGraw
- Tom Brady
- The Rock
- Theory
- James Perse
- Rhone
- GREATS
- RAEN
- VRB Labs
- LMNT
- Athletic Greens
- Huron
- Concept 2
- Land Rover
- Omega
- Onnit
- XPT
- Porsche 911

CHAPTER 24

ROI or ROL?

Simplifying things gives you better
quality on what you retain.

*Being a minimalist to me means thinking about what I want
with my time. If I wanted more things, I needed to sacrifice more time to acquire those things. And that's something
I didn't want to do. I wanted to focus more on doing things
than owning things. I'm kind of a weird person in this sense.
People make fun of me all the time for how I want to live.
Like I have a dream to live in a hotel for a little bit. That to
me is very minimalist. You can't really have a lot of things
if you want to move around. I like to be mobile. I like to be
able to go where I want to go for as long as I want to go.
I cannot focus on possessions. I feel like after a while they*

start to weigh me down. I realized too that a lot of the things I've bought, I'm excited about them for a couple weeks, maybe a couple months, and then after a while you get over it. Again, converting money into time, this is extra time I have to spend working to buy what I want to buy, and I just didn't want to get into that cycle.

I feel like once I detached myself from a feeling for things, I was able to focus more on things I actually do and not what I own. This all stemmed from a trip I took back in 2012. I hiked Mt. Kilimanjaro with a bunch of friends of mine and sustained myself for three weeks with just whatever was in my backpack. I had the time of my life. One of the best trips I've ever taken. When I came back into my apartment, I almost felt overwhelmed with all the things I had. I started taking a closer look and thought, "Man, I don't use half this stuff, and I just spent three of the best weeks of my life with just what was on my back." That set in motion for me this thought of minimalizing and simplifying what I needed to be happy and sustain myself.

I try to keep it basic with what I wear. I guess I did have a little bit of a clothes fascination when I was working in corporate America. I had nice shoes, nice shirts, nice ties, but that was part of that double life I felt. I didn't feel very comfortable in that stuff after a while, and as soon as I got home, I'd tear it all off anyway.

Creating that emotional detachment from things has really helped me. I started having these thoughts and started looking at books to read and websites and blogs to follow. I came across this book, Everything That Remains. I read that and I was like, "Holy hell, this is exactly the path I'm on!" It was mainly thinking about people and experiences as opposed to owning more things. Their concept is owning more things almost creates a little prison cell for you. Your possessions own you after a while.

— **BRIAN GALLAGHER,** cofounder of Throwback Fitness and author of *Simple Man Guide*, on *The Midlife Male* podcast, Episode #25

* * *

I don't typically spend a lot of time talking or thinking about money, which I suppose is a good problem to have. I am far from a minimalist, but I do respect the ethos and embrace it at times, probably more so as I get older and not always for the most consistent of reasons. I don't spend a lot of money on alcohol, but that's more an investment in the morning after than any grand earth-loving purpose. I drink Strong brand coffee like it's liquid honey from the gods, and I have no plans to step back from that daily pleasure.

With growing kids and their activities, along with my love of brand-name watches, sneakers, and fitness tech, I plunk down money pretty regularly. Kate reins me in somewhat, but she also contributes to our expense sheet, including a love for cooking equipment, plants, and anything that can be used to organize a house or room.

Whether you spend a lot or a little, paying attention to your budget and where you want your hard-earned money to go is essential for all of us. If the COVID-19 pandemic wasn't reason enough for you to home in on what you really value, just keep in mind that the clock is ticking for each of us. The economy is uncertain for all of us. The best

can take is clearly naming what we want to pri-
ᵣ ourselves and those closest to us.

᧐ in stressful times, such as the 2020 quarantine or
tᵢₓ ₑeat Recession before that, I look at the future opti-
mistically. Actually, in part because of those stressful times,
I'm optimistic. They force us to pay attention and make
course corrections in our lives.

We're all familiar with the term ROI: return on investment.

What about ROL: return on life?

It is important to balance return on investments with
return on life. Wealth manager Jeff Griswold defines ROL
as "how well you are doing in living the life you want with
the money you have."

Return on Life: "How well you are doing in living the life
you want with the money you have."

—JEFF GRISWOLD, wealth manager

What I like about this definition is that it doesn't com-
pare you to anybody else, and it doesn't assume anything
about your stage of life, your financial status, or even your
financial aspirations. It focuses on quality as *you* define it
given *your* specific situation.

Griswold provides these key ROL indicators:

- Living well within your means
- Investing time, energy, and resources in people and
  engagements that energize you

- Allowing yourself to have experiences and fulfillment whenever possible
- Not comparing yourself to others who may live with a different set of circumstances
- Living purposefully
- Not allowing your identity to be defined by numbers

Henry David Thoreau, who knew a thing or two about living sustainably (and as far as I know never had difficulty saying no to a new pair of sneakers), once said, "The price of anything is the amount of life you exchange for it."

The amount of *life* you exchange for something. That could be money earned by time you spent working. It could be mental anxiety (or positive mental exertion) that you devoted toward something. The point is: you're paying every day with your time, skills, and money. How will you allocate those assets for the best return on the investment of your time on this planet?

That's where I feel like I do align with the minimalist mindset. You need to simplify to the degree that creates maximum happiness for you, and it's clear to me that happiness is higher in people who prioritize healthy relationships and meaningful experiences. If you can reduce clutter to spend more energy on those two items, you'll have a healthy ROL.

This is not a one-and-done deal either. Just as you don't write your will and then never reassess it, you don't decide you've reached your level of sustainability and stop paying attention. Your needs, wants, dreams, and responsibilities will change. Your definitions of success and legacy could change.

All of that impacts your ROL. In many ways, your ROL is the most important financial term you'll ever confront, so make sure you control the dividends.

Get Iconic

Simplify yourself

You don't need to be passionate about EVERY decision. How much time do you spend making decisions on things that don't matter? What shirt you're going to wear? Where you're going out to eat and then what you're choosing from the menu once you're there? What beer to buy? What movie to stream? There's nothing wrong with finding what works for you and taking the choice out of your own hands some of the time.

Cull the closet. You don't have to go full Thoreau to make an impact on the space you require for your clothes. You can have style without massive expense. Invest in the clothing that you feel good in, and make it your uniform. Find clothes that serve multiple purposes rather than having fifteen different go-to looks. Take a month to get rid of one thing every day; that's thirty fewer things to deal with when you're done.

Buy one, drop one. Whenever you buy one thing, require yourself to get rid of something else.

Pure foods. Buy foods that have very few ingredients. They're healthier for you and require far fewer resources to get them to your door.

Keep your workouts simple. I geek out on fitness equipment and gadgets, but you don't have to spend a ton of money to be physically fit. Find bars at a park and do pull-ups. If you don't do anything more than sit-ups, push-ups, squats, and walking, you'll be set. If you can't squat, then just bend a little. You're not going to the Olympics with this regimen, but who the fuck is? You won't die at your desk, and your wife will still want to fuck you. I'd call that a win.

Portraits and Life

My son and I got portraits taken by the amazing photographer and artist Jay Rusovich.

We get so used to seeing images on our phones, iPads, and pretty much any screen that it's hard to appreciate the detail, clarity, and creativity that go into portrait photography.

You have to get close to the photograph and spend time with it to experience it fully.

Kinda like life.

The Sixth F
FUN

- ☐ Do you know who you are?
- ☐ If you could live anywhere, where would it be?
- ☐ Who and what inspires you?
- ☐ What fills your tank?
- ☐ What activity have you never taken up that you still want to?
- ☐ When is your next vacation?
- ☐ What does fun even mean to you?
- ☐ Have you stopped having fun, or are you having too much of it?
- ☐ Why does the word "fun" seem to have been taken out of our vocabulary?
- ☐ Would your friends describe you as a fun person?
- ☐ What would you like to bring back into your life that would be fun?

CHAPTER 25

The Clock Is Ticking . . .
Take Your Shot

Be conscious of how you spend your time.

When my brother died, I was working as a trainer at Bally Total Fitness. I was twenty-two years old and in incredible physical shape. I was no longer playing soccer. I was training like a professional athlete but with no competition, nothing to put my heart into. When my brother passed away, I had just heard this ad on the radio for a fight in a tournament: the Milwaukee Rumble. I got the call at five in the morning that my brother had died from a drug overdose. I drove over to the site. I was not able to see my brother's body. That hit me in a certain way that I couldn't deal with. I got into a pushing match with a sheriff. I was told to leave before I got arrested.

So I drove to Hal's Harley-Davidson, and I signed up for this fight. Two weeks later, I stepped into a ring with a kid who had no idea what he was walking into because of the amount of rage that I had flowing through me. He was six foot four, 230 pounds. I was five eleven, 205. They're like, "Are you sure you don't want to cut a pound? You'd be a lighter weight." I'm like, "Nope, whatever." I knocked this kid out in fifteen seconds, unconscious. Next fight, same thing. Next night, I ended up losing, but that's when it all began. I had a guy grab me, and he said, "I see your anger. I see what's going on. I mean, I don't know what's going on, but I see something going on. I can do something with this. I can channel this." He took me under his wing. He was a martial artist. He started training me, and his passion and dedication of wanting to work with me, and my fascination with physical performance, that connected it, and I was sold. I didn't need any conversation. There was no interest in money, just the pure feeling of it. At that moment, I needed to feel something, because I didn't feel anything when my brother died. Physical movement, fighting, weightlifting, whatever it was, it saved me at that moment.

There was this moment at his death, sometime between him dying and me signing the paperwork for that fight within a couple hours, this kind of metaphorical shot clock in the corner of my eye appeared. It's fuzzy, but it's moving. And you know it's not going up; it's going down. And every time I try to turn to it, it's always in the corner of my eye. So, because I don't know how much time is on it, I'm going to do what any person is going to do with the ball when the shot clock is about to be out. I'm going to shoot the ball. I've always taken the shot. I like to say yes to things that I feel like *are going to teach me something or advance me in some way that makes sense to my core ideas.*

— **ADAM VON ROTHFELDER,** founder of Strong Coffee Company, former MMA fighter, personal trainer, and fashion and fitness model, on *The Midlife Male* podcast, Episode #94

* * *

If you know me at all, you know that I stress two things: grab life by the balls and make the most of every day you're blessed to receive on this earth. And . . . chill out and don't overbook your life.

Both of these exhortations can be true.

There's what you want or need that you say yes to, and there's what you don't want or need that you say no to. Where it becomes dicey is when you want or need something that you say no to and what you don't want or need that you say yes to. Then you're in the realm of obligations and opportunity costs and FOMO. I can't sort all that out for you. What I can tell you is that if you develop a strong sense of who you want to be and who you are, these questions become a lot easier. At the core of deciding who you want to be by the time you're gone is respecting the fact that you will be gone. Someday, you'll be gone. Because the shot clock is ticking. Whether you choose to be busy or not, you're not going to be able to stop the clock. Life doesn't give you a series of time-outs.

Doing less but with more focus

I posted a video from my band rehearsal. That evening I got a message from a guy saying, "What don't you do?"

The truth is *a lot*.

I don't do *a lot*.

I used to do *a lot* more. It's taken me *a lot* of time to cut back, streamline, figure out what's important, who's important, where I want to commit time, who I want to spend time with, what I truly enjoy doing—and more importantly, what I don't.

I strive now to do less but with more focus. That's at the core of everything for me. That's where authenticity, true success, and fulfillment really come into play.

Why would I stop playing guitar and playing in a band? I love it.

Why would I stop exercising? It feels great.

Why would I stop podcasting? It's unbelievably enlightening.

Why would I stop blogging? It's therapeutic.

Why would I stop being in businesses that help people? It's provided a very nice lifestyle and meaningful relationships.

Why would I stop spending every moment I can with my family? They're the best part of my life.

Jay Shetty, an author, life coach, and former monk, once wrote, "Find three hobbies. One to make you money, one to keep you in shape, and one to keep you creative." He nailed it. That's really it. Go back and look at my list above. With the exception of family, which always comes first, I'm doing my best to stick to that mantra.

Stick to your rules

What is difficult for many of us who think we're still twenty-four years old and can do it all is imposing rules on ourselves and then sticking to them. By the time you're in midlife, I hope you learn the benefits of *not* doing certain things so that you can afford to do the things that you do do. Got that?

* I don't stay out late.
* I don't really drink anymore.
* I don't sleep in.
* I don't play golf.
* I don't take four-hour bike rides or jogs.
* I don't live in my office.
* I don't go to parties or events that I don't want to.
* I don't coach my son's teams any longer.
* I don't watch a lot of TV, movies, or even sports.
* I don't watch or read much news.
* I don't talk or give my time to people or business that I don't want to.

Believe me, this is really fucking hard. Particularly at first, because adopting a lot of the above involved major fundamental changes to my lifestyle and decision-making process. It comes down to discipline, strength, willingness to change, and beginning to get comfortable with being uncomfortable.

You have to fight the fear of missing out, or being labeled a quitter, or losing some friends, or pissing off some people. What you create in this process, though, is the ability to play the long game toward sustainability, longevity, authenticity, vulnerability, security, and contentment. Gradually the changes and commitment result in feeling and acting better and becoming more secure and comfortable in your own skin. You reduce the FOMO because what you're already doing is where you know you want to be. You upgrade from those who weren't adding to your life or appreciating your value to surrounding yourself with more like-minded and positive relationships.

You really free up a lot of time when you *don't* do a lot of things. Start saying no, or just simply stop showing up to the stuff you don't need to be involved with.

Tips to take control of what you do

Some of the steps I've taken that have helped me get to this place are:

- Replace dinners and drinks with workouts and breakfasts.

- Replace people and clients who require dinners and drinks with people who prefer workouts and breakfasts. (For some this may not be as realistic, but the key is to strive to create more overall balance.)

- I don't drink when I go out. I allow myself to have a drink or two at home. I have much greater self-control this way, and cutting out alcohol altogether was not something I've been able to do.

- Set boundaries and expectations. When I do need to go out to something in the evenings, I put it out there up front what time I must leave because I have a workout or meeting in the morning.

- We cut out our cable and went to Apple TV (with streaming services Netflix and Amazon Prime), so we don't have the mindless channel surfing going on like we used to. This also saved more than $200 a month!

- I picked two or three boards, events, leagues, and organizations that I wanted to be part of, and then I said *no* to everything else. Most important here is that when people ask for you to be part of something or give your time and/or money, you must say, "I am committed to this, this, and this currently, so please check back with me next year when I reevaluate."

- Put everything on the calendar! Workouts, meetings, podcast recordings, kids' practices/games, band practices. Then it becomes easier to see where you're overloaded, overcommitted, or have time to do that thing you really want to do.

- Stop looking at what everyone else is doing. Really, just don't look. IG, FB . . . you're not going to keep up with multiple lives or the posts. Be the content producer, not the consumer. If you're really into it, find a few people on social media that motivate and inspire you to be better.

You can *do* this. You can *do* more or less. It's up to *you*.

For Chrissakes, schedule something already
Take the lead. Guys don't schedule anything. They don't follow through. More generally, there are few people whom you can count on to do what they say they're going to do or are even on time. That shouldn't be a hard fucking benchmark. But it is rare.

Schedule an adult get-together that doesn't include going to a gym: Watch *Fight Club* with your guys, and bring the snacks. Make a reservation for a double date with your partner and another couple. Get creative.

Be the guy who makes shit happen.

If It's Not Fun, Then I'm Done

We all have to do things in life that we don't enjoy. That's why it's called work. I don't care how passionate you are about your job, fitness, anything. Some aspect of it sucks. Do it anyway.

However, one of the reasons people don't stick to things is because they're not having fun. Find activities, people, places, projects, positions (I'm referring to jobs/careers here, but you can fill in the blank), and products that put a smile on your face.

CHAPTER 26
Embrace the Suck

Discipline isn't fun, but it's the key
to accomplishing great things.

Queer Eye *showed up to film seasons three and four in Kansas City, and they were living in a building right next to my gym, so they all got gym memberships. Antoni [Porowski], the food and wine guy on the show, was working out and he was finished, and I just went over and introduced myself and told him I'm one of the trainers here and that I grew up here. I gave him recommendations for a couple of restaurants to check out. It wasn't immediately trying to sell training. It was "welcome to town." He said, "Let's set up a session and get in a workout," so we set something up for the next morning. The other guys came up and said, "Antoni mentioned you." I ended up training a few of them while they were there.*

They went back to LA or New York or wherever they live. I was going to keep training and building my business, and a few weeks after they left, Bobby [Berk] texted me. He said, "Hey, would you ever consider moving to LA?" I was like, "Yeah." We talked on the phone, and he knew I had been a chef. He said that he wanted somebody to be his trainer in LA and do home workouts because their schedules are all over the place. He wanted to set up a home gym and have me come over and train him and be his personal chef and do all his meal prep and cooking. He was getting ready to launch his lifestyle blog and wanted someone to do fitness and food content for the site. He was like, "If you move to LA, I get a trainer, a chef, and someone for my website. Instead of having to hire three people, I only have to hire one."

When I moved out to LA, I decided I was going to take up surfing. It had been a while since I had done something physically that was difficult for me. I had been working out for a while, doing powerlifting in the CrossFit space. I had reached a point where the games were a little slower. Being a beginner at something—sucking at something—having to really build yourself up, that mindset will translate into everything else.

Whenever I've found myself in that position where I get a little complacent, I go be a beginner at something. Everyone likes doing things they're good at. You've got a job, you're good at it. You know what you're doing. Maybe it's fitness. You've been doing the same thing and reached this point where you're plateaued but you're comfortable. Finding something where you're a beginner, it can switch your mindset and everything else as well.

I just started training for my first triathlon. Coming from strength-training sports, triathlon is not my strong suit. Any-

thing endurance is not my strong suit, but it's fun being a beginner at something. There's two sides to fun. There's enjoying the activity where you're enjoying the whole process and not worried about the result. But there's also the rewarding aspect of fun. Training for this triathlon, I'm not enjoying every moment. I'm not enjoying the running. But it's rewarding. I'm having fun in the process. It's finding the balance. Have fun, but know you're not enjoying every moment.

— **ZACH MORGAN,** chef, trainer, and health and wellness expert, on *The Midlife Male* podcast, Episode #143

* * *

You're going to suck a lot more running away from the suck than if you invite the suck in and show him you're not afraid. That's right: him. I envision "the Suck" as an irritating dude bug—a real douchebag, with beady eyes, thick eyebrows, and a fat, furry body with stick arms and legs—that keeps telling you how bad you are at your relationships, your job, your intelligence, your athletic skills, your time management, your parenting decisions, everything. And he won't leave until you force him to leave.

How do you force him to leave? You keep inviting him back for more punishment that *you* are dishing out. Embracing the suck can be about trying something you're going to suck at because it's new, or it can be about embracing something you don't like to do but needs to get done. If it's the former, you'll embrace the suck of trying something new because that's how you improve at something. If the latter, you'll embrace it because then you can move on to the next task or fun thing you've got on the list.

Often, the two are intertwined. It requires discipline—external or internal—to get better at something or to get your shit done. It's simple to embrace the Suck, but it's not easy. We fool ourselves into thinking we can escape the Suck entirely:

- We think, "I'm going to quit my job and turn my hobby into my profession." Guess what: a sexier vocation doesn't mean some of it doesn't suck. You're still looking at spreadsheets. You're still fielding complaints. You're still watching an assembly line of employees complain about their life or their coworker.

- We commit paralysis by analysis, reading and listening to how to maximize our life without actually doing the work to make it happen. When you start to work on it, you realize the Suck is lurking, because the pursuit of happiness doesn't mean you're happy all the freakin' time. Sometimes you have to punch the Suck in the nose to get there.

- We say, "I'm going to hire the best personal trainer and have the best workout program assigned to me," even though "the best" includes all the exercises I hate in a setting I don't like. You know what the best workout program is? The one you enjoy the most. That's the one you're not going to coast through. That's the one where you won't skip days. If you don't enjoy one activity, try another. If you don't like the next one, try another. Think you'll exhaust all the possibilities? Trust me, you won't. It's a long damn list. Eventually, you'll wear out "the Suck" in your quest.

I struggle with doing the things that I know I have to do and don't want to. Just the word *discipline* has negative connotations for me. It brings back memories of being told what to do, of getting scolded, criticized, talked down to, and punished.

When something is negative or makes you feel bad, you tend to run away from it. Plus, it's usually hard, either physically, mentally, emotionally, or spiritually. Getting ourselves to do what's hard is, well . . . hard.

So how do we learn to embrace the suck?

One thing that's worked for me is to replace the notion of being disciplined with behavior I can be proud of—being consistent and having self-control. It feels better. It's more positive. Plus, we *are what we repeatedly do*. If I'm consistent and practice self-control with something, I usually end up being pretty good at it over time; if I feel controlled or forced, I rebel or fight it.

Some people like discipline, and if that's what you need, go for it. Whatever works for you. We're all motivated differently. For some people, rigid and scheduled works; for others it's crippling. Some can handle and thrive on the consistency of inconsistency. They move fluidly from one activity and obligation to another, completing tasks when they feel motivated, not beholden to deadline.

Discipline is nothing more than the habit of consistency—finding the motivation to do something again and again until you do it on autopilot and start seeing results. And it crops up in all areas of life.

Writing

I write a weekly newsletter. I enjoy doing it. I'm not obligated to do it, but it provides not only a creative outlet and mental exercise but a consistent schedule. That means that if I have to put this out on Sunday morning, then I really can't be out late on Saturday. So there's my excuse to leave the event or party early or not go out at all. I built a system that helps *me*, and it becomes easier to adhere to over time. Is that a form of discipline? Yes, but in my mind it's more about consistency and self-control. It doesn't really matter if I send out the newsletter at 11:00 a.m. instead of 9:00 a.m. I don't beat myself up over it or hold myself to that rigid standard. I've simply built parameters I can work within.

Workouts

Now, if you moved my workouts to 5:00 a.m., then I'd need some real discipline. I wouldn't like it. I'm not a superearly riser, don't perform well at that hour, and am not willing to change at this stage of my life. Sure, every once in a while I do it, but not consistently. I don't have that degree of self-control. My consistency is based around my being able to commit to certain times, not being forced to conform to one time.

Work

With business I adhere to a much stricter schedule. Renewal dates are firm. Marketing timeframes are firm. Response times are critical. I work hard on having that self-control.

Other aspects, such as meeting with clients, discussing their businesses and risks, and designing and implementing their programs, are exciting; the minutiae of policy forms, invoicing, and logistics are challenging. I've built a support system around those areas where I can delegate and still maintain the level of self-control and consistency to stay on top of what is important.

The biggest challenge is to stay focused and maintain self-control when there are so many things competing for your time.

Embrace the small stuff

Once I'm done with my routine, such as it is—working out, recovery, writing, meditating, eating (all the things I like)—do I possess the self-control to sit down and answer every client email, read the policy forms I need to, dig into that work comp audit, respond to the claim issue that I know is going to suck, do taxes? We all have aspects of our jobs and lives that we enjoy and gravitate toward more than others. This is about how we manage the other side of the ledger.

In "A Guide to Developing the Self-Discipline Habit," Leo Babauta writes, "One of the most important things you can do to get better at self-discipline is to take small actions. It can seem overwhelming to tackle huge, intimidating projects . . . so don't. Instead, tackle easy actions, things so small you can't say no."

Have some taxes to do? Just do five minutes.

Want to run? Just run for ten minutes.

Have a report to work on? Just do the first few paragraphs.

Want to declutter? Just find five things to declutter.

The superpower of self-control

People with a higher degree of self-control spend less time debating whether to indulge in behaviors that are detrimental to their health and are able to make positive decisions more easily. They don't let impulses or feelings dictate their choices. Instead, they make levelheaded decisions. As a result, they tend to feel more satisfied with their lives. According to a University of Chicago research team that studied the effects of self-control on life satisfaction, this is the case in the short term as well as the long term.

Wilhelm Hofmann, who led the team, called self-control "among humankind's most valuable assets."

So just try embracing the suck, one small task at a time, pushing yourself into discomfort. See how it feels. See that it's not the end of the world. See that you are awesome enough to handle discomfort, and that the results are well worth it.

Get Moving

One thing

Do *one* amazing thing for yourself every day.

Wait, you thought there'd be more to this?

No.

Just try it for thirty days, and see how much better everything gets.

It can be as little as adding five minutes of meditation a day. Writing someone a note. Taking a walk. Allowing yourself to eat that peach tart for breakfast. Helping someone with their bags. Solving a client's

issue. Going for a swim. Cutting out that toxic person. Playing with your dog. Trying out a new look.
  You're worth it.

Between the Highlights

You know what social media posts and newsletters of mine get the most reaction?

The lowlights.

It's easy to show the highlights, and I have a lot to be grateful for. I always strive to accentuate the positive.

But the reality is there are just as many lowlights, if not more, and what you don't see and what I don't always show are the losses, anxieties, trials, and tribulations that make up the majority of the time.

I think it's really important to not only show your best moments. Part of maximizing middle age is being able to work through the low moments—to own them and share them as unapologetically as you share the highlight reel.

So when you see me in my best shape physically, consider that I may be feeling my worst and overcompensating. Or that often when I'm a little less in shape, I'm likely much happier overall and things are going better in a lot of other areas.

Maybe we all need something called "Between the Highlights" that falls short of the airbrushed, curated, perceived perfection of a post and somewhere above the dog-shit-on-the-carpet or I'm-in-bed-with-the-flu realities of life. Or maybe we include those too.

The point is I'm talking about a place where we can share what's not working. That's where you really learn and grow—from the mistakes, failures, rejections, decisions, and choices you made that weren't so good. It's what you do from there that really matters.

It's exhausting to just see highlights. Even ESPN's web gems get boring after a while.

I can't keep up with trying to make my own and certainly can't keep up with scrolling through multiple people's highlights and thinking that's good for my sanity and well-being.

I want to talk about it.

I want to write about it.

Let's spend more time between the highlights.

In (Men)tal Health,
—Greg

CHAPTER 27
Do Your Calisthenics

Take care of preparation and the little things.

I didn't know where to start seven or eight years ago, and the reason I'm saying there's seven or eight years ago even though there's seven summits is I had to go back to Denali, which is the highest peak in North America. It's a mother. I didn't make it the first time. It was minus eighty at the top and minus forty where my camp was. When I first researched how to even pull this thing off [climbing the Seven Summits], I reached out to some people I knew out of Seattle who owned mountaineering, adventure-climbing companies who actually do this and guide people around the world to take this on. I called them up and said, "This is what I'm looking to do." They'd done the Seven several times, and they gave me the planogram. I always thought, "Oh, there's a mountain, I'm going to go climb it," and that's it. What I didn't factor in was all the variables that come into it, the weather for sure. Something else where I really had to hone my game was learning the nutrition end, hydration, the right kinds of food. The higher you get on the mountain, your appetite gets suppressed. You're burning tons of calories and you don't want to eat, but you have to keep feeding the machine. And the last part of that is what to wear. We call it self-care on the mountain. When it's freezing out and you've been hiking up a steep pitch, you have to know what to put on, when to put it on, and how to react.

I was with a guy down in Antarctica. We were climbing a mountain called Mt. Benson. This guy had been on Denali, actually, six months before we hooked up. We were within three days of each other summiting. He summitted it first. He lost three fingers and part of his nose on Denali, and now I'm tent-mating with him down in Benson. We were all concerned because he just did not have great self-care. He was losing gloves and hats and water bottles. He was just a mess. A year later, when you saw all those big lineups on Mt. Everest, he got caught up in all that. You know, he's not a very fast climber, took forever just to get to the top, got to the top, raised his hand, fell over dead. He's still sitting up there now. We could see this coming. Going back to John Wooden's Pyramid of Success, you have Competitive Greatness at the top. You have to love the process and everything that leads up to it—which I don't think that guy did. I think he wanted to be known as the cool guy that climbed Mt. Everest, but he didn't love the process like I do of training by going up and down the mountain when no one else is around, no camera action, any of that stuff.

Metaphorically speaking, when you're climbing mountains, whether it's business, relationships, anything else, it's about keep learning, keep growing, keep putting one foot in front of the other as you climb that mountain. If you don't love it, there's just too many reasons to quit. Then, when you start playing on a mountain like Everest, and it's literally life-and-death stakes on the table, you end up with failed results like what happened to him.

— **MARK PATTISON,** entrepreneur, philanthropist, retired NFL player, and climber of the Seven Summits, on *The Midlife Male* podcast, Episode #107

* * *

You don't have to climb the world's highest mountain to know the lure of sports and physical activity. It's a rush to just stay fit. It's an even greater feat to push it and still be competitive both in the gym and in an adventure race or a boxing ring—not that I'm going to take a round from Lennox Lewis. You've just gotta find things that move the needle for you.

But if you're only participating in physical activity to get a certain look or gain bragging rights or for the ego boost of a win, you're going to have a problem continuing when something gets in your way—an injury, your schedule, an unforeseen change. Ultimately, you've got to enjoy the process. You need to choose what is fun. It's not any more complicated than that.

Remember doing old-school calisthenics in gym class? I didn't enjoy doing those simple exercises, and I'm pretty sure my gym teacher didn't explain why we had to waste time doing them before we could get started on tetherball or scooters or dodgeball or whatever the hell else we played back then. (Yeah, I played dodgeball, and I liked it. If you can dodge a wrench, you can dodge a ball!) Those exercises seemed meaningless, but they actually prepared our bodies for the work ahead and kept us from getting injured. They were a form of self-care. I do calisthenics of a different kind every day now. These are exercises that help manifest the life that I want: purpose, focus, simplicity, authenticity, contentment. A series of little things done consistently over time results in big changes.

Hey, I procrastinate. I do too many things at one time. I'm easily distracted. I'm temperamental. I get frustrated quickly. I say too much. I'm guilty of negative self-talk and comparing myself to others. I have confidence issues, social anxiety, body image insecurity, relationship challenges, and trouble relaxing. I get injured constantly and have the stereotypical Jewish guilt, and yet, in spite of it all . . . I'm truly very fortunate and have a great life. I love my family, friends, and my dog. I cherish my health and my career, laugh a lot, and eat well.

The reason I can say all of this and be all of this is because I'm doing my calisthenics. I don't sweat that stuff all that often anymore.

"Where awareness goes, energy flows."

—GURUDEVA

As I was driving home from getting a tire fixed on Kate's car one time, it started raining. Now, let me preface this by saying that I really didn't want to have to go to the tire store. It was annoying that a brand-new car with fresh tires now had a nail in it and that I had to get up off the couch (I was watching *Invincible*, for crying out loud . . . I love that movie!) and go get this done. But I begrudgingly did it because I was told to. It wasn't going to fix itself, and now I could go home and tell Kate what a good husband I was and do my little "I'm great" dance instead of saying what I really wanted to say, which was "Why don't you go do this on Monday while I'm at work?" (Cue couple's argument . . . three, two, one . . . go.)

Back to the rain, which is what's most important here. As it was pouring and I was driving home in the new car, with the new tire, dry as can be, I passed a family standing at the bus stop: mother, father, baby carriage, and another daughter probably around seven years old. They were outside, getting drenched, no umbrella, and waiting for the bus.

My energy flowed to being grateful to have the new car, the means to buy the new tire, for being dry, for not having to take the bus. My awareness shifted away from all that negative stuff running through my head . . . Yeah, it kind of surprised me too.

Despite the Insta life we all get fed, we shouldn't be just striving for the peaks. We need to respect the process along the way, and that includes some valleys too. Responsibilities, compromises . . . these aren't bad things. They help us grow.

rious

vn personal gym class

Here is a list of the ten calisthenics that I'm currently working on—call it my own personal midlife male gym class. I say "working on" because I don't nail every one of these every day.

1. Have a morning routine. Mine involves getting up before the rest of my family. I make coffee with vital proteins; drink a huge glass of water with Athletic Greens, creatine, and BCAAs; take a bath with Epsom salts and meditate; then read and send emails. This sets me up for the day.

2. Reread your goals. I have my goals on paper— personal, professional, financial, health, family, travel. And I read them, daily. It helps me stay focused, motivated, and reminded of where I want to go.

3. Do "one" thing per day. I write down three things that I need to get done. That's why the "one" is in quotes. I certainly hope we can do more than one thing in a day, but you know . . . some days are better than others. Then I do the first one. If this takes all day, then that's all I'll do. But if I finish, then I'll move on to numbers two and three. The key is that you can't move on until you've finished the task before.

4. Invoke the twenty-four-hour rule. Once upon a time, I was the king of the immediate, emotional, and often regrettable response. Now, I have a rule

that I write it, *but* . . . I wait twenty-four hours before sending. Everything can wait twenty-four hours, especially something that could have big consequences in my relationships or results if I let my emotions dictate my reply. I'll reread it the next day, check myself, and ensure that I'm cool with actually sending it.

5. Check in with your accountability coach. You're going to have days where you lack motivation, can't get moving, aren't doing what you said you were going to do. You need someone for support when this happens. Find an accountability coach. This is someone you can call, or better yet who calls you, during the week and keeps you moving forward and on your game.

6. Stop saying "I can't" and "I'll try." It's all in your thoughts. This calisthenic is particularly important. Be careful about what you are saying and thinking to yourself. Your thoughts are what you become. Only can, never can't. Only do or won't do, never "I'll try." You can self-impose a five-dollar fine on yourself every time you use one of these forbidden sentences, and donate the pot to a charity above and beyond what you normally give. Perhaps you donate it to a new charity.

7. Work your plan. You made the plan, right? Keep working it. Consistency is the key. Get up, show up, put in the work. You didn't miss your opportunity. You just didn't create your opportunity.

8. Exercise. PE calisthenics still apply. Want to decrease stress, be happier, look better, feel better, move better, live longer, sleep better, and have more energy, strength, and endurance? This is a no-brainer.

9. Understand your end code. This is all about knowing who you are. Coming back to center, not getting pulled into situations, places, people, and jobs that don't align with your true self. You'll be continually tested on this one.

10. Practice. Whatever we practice, we get good at. Simple as it gets.

It takes discipline to do the calisthenics. Discipline equals freedom, and freedom equals fulfillment.

I'm Back from Vacation . . .

Just wanted to shed some light on how appearances on vacations may (and actually do) differ from reality.

I am a deal shopper. Booked this on Expedia.

I wake up early, we go out and do activities all day and pretty much only see the inside of a room to sleep, so paying exorbitant room rates gives me a stomachache.

We stay in one room. The four of us. It's tight.

We have other plans coming up and other expenses, so if we want to spend a week in Laguna, this is how I can do it.

It's a good thing we all love each other very much.

I don't buy drinks in a hotel or at a restaurant. Granted, I don't drink very much anyway, but I won't pay that markup and Kate drinks, so that's our compromise.

I did buy a small bottle of Don Julio silver tequila for thirty bucks. It lasted me the entire time I was out there. A few years ago, it would have lasted all of two hours.

I do believe in spending on great food and finding new restaurants wherever we go. I can't stand being let down by bad food or spending hotel prices for mediocre food.

My preference is to always spend on experiences over things, so yes, we did the whale-watching tour and rented a Jeep to drive up Pacific Coast Highway, and I consider our hotel and its location right on the cliff and the ocean an experience.

I always work on vacation. I get up before everybody gets up, send my emails, make my phone calls, write . . . whatever I need to do for work, because in order for me to have a clear head and enjoy the day with my family, I have to knock all of this stuff out.

This particular trip I did not work out. My body needed a break, so the most I did was walk with Kate each morning. The boys slept in.

We have typical "problems of prosperity" that I don't take pics of because my kids hate it, but I snuck a few in.

Kate's TSA PreCheck didn't work, which was clearly my fault because I booked the tickets.

We stood around waiting for Ubers on multiple occasions because apparently Uber is not great out there in Dana Point, and I think my rating has gone down due to a bunch of canceled trips in Chicago.

It wasn't bad; I'm not complaining. I'm fortunate to be able to do this. Just sayin' . . .

#family #reality #dad #accountability #health #perseverance #experience

CHAPTER 28

Are You Ready for an Environment Shift?

Change your location to keep from getting stuck in a rut.

The first thing I do when I need to get my mojo back is look at my environment. That could be my work environment, could be the home environment, but I think mostly it's the people you surround yourself with. Being more proactive about surrounding yourself with people who either you want to emulate or you like their habits or routines. I know when I'm stuck in a rut, I'm probably not spending enough time around people who are trying to grow their business, people who are trying to be healthy, people who are trying to do things in their life.

So the first thing I do is an environment shift. I go through my phone. Who can I have coffee with this week? Who is just super exciting and doing big things with their business, their life, their health, or their family? Who can I just talk to? Is it a friend, is it a fellow entrepreneur, is it someone from the fitness side, is it a pastor? Who is it that I can get around so I can change the people I'm around so that I can catch some of their vibe? Who can I have coffee with? Who can I have a juice with? Who can I walk around the park with and just get my mind into the right frame? That will start the process of getting you out of that rut. I know that as soon as I get into a rut, that comfort zone, I look at my schedule over the past thirty days and I'll be like, "Man, I've just been going to the office, hanging out by myself. I haven't been surrounding myself with anybody with positive energy," and that's a quick culprit to why I'm in that rut in the first place.

I change my environment. If it's work, I do a lot of creative writing, video work, and media. If I'm staring at a blank screen, the first thing I do is change locations. Leave the sterile office, go to the coffee shop, or go sit outside. Luckily, I live in beautiful Florida, and it's pretty much ninety degrees every day of the year, so I can sweat it out outside with a cold brew and I can write somewhere. Changing that physical environment and the people that you're around, that is the number one thing you can do. That's a quick fix. That's not going to a Tony Robbins seven-day seminar. That's not buying a course online. It's something you can do this afternoon.

— **GREG ROLLETT,** host, *The Daily Ambition with Greg Rollett* and *Dad Chat* podcasts, on *The Midlife Male* podcast, Episode #98

* * *

Making an environment shift can be done with people—I get a weekly escape from my rut when I enter the worlds of my podcast guests, who are always people who are "super exciting and doing big things with their business, their life, their health, or their family."

Or an environment shift can be done alone. I happen to like being by myself. Not all the time; I crave the energy of family and friends. But if you don't like being by yourself, you should consider why. Part of being a good friend and family member is also the self-reflection and replenishing time that goes with time alone, whether on a walk, a run, a drive, a meditation, reading . . . even work.

Take the back roads

I needed to be in San Antonio for business a while back. On the drive from Austin to San Antonio, I just plugged the destination into my Waze and started driving. Somewhere along the way, I got rerouted due to traffic and ended up on some farm-to-market back roads. Once I got over being annoyed by being delayed and having no idea where I was, I started to enjoy the ride, the scenery, and the alone time.

Instead of being on a crowded, nondescript highway, I was winding my way through beautiful farmland and ranches, with more cows and horses than I could count. All that livestock may not exactly be as thrilling as seeing hundreds of zebras and elephants in the Serengeti. But it provided the serenity and solitude at that moment that I didn't even know I needed.

We tend to move so quickly. We are constantly on the go, looking for the fastest route. And for what? When was the last time you:

- got in your car and just drove?
- went out for a meal by yourself and didn't rush through it?
- attended a movie, show, or event by yourself?
- just took a solo walk?
- swam in cold water?
- took a (nonbusiness) trip by yourself?

Sometimes just taking the back roads is all you need to change your mood.

Take your workout outside

If you want to change your perspective or upgrade your mindset, the number one best way I've found is to get outside. It's that simple.

Your outlook is directly correlated to the amount of time you spend outdoors.

Start by getting out in the sunshine and taking advantage of beautiful days. Feel the grass beneath your feet, and soak in the blue sky above. Before long, you may find that rainy days or cloud watching becomes your thing.

Take a walk around the block. Use the field at your local rec center. Put a few movements together. If you begin to consistently start or end your day this way, it'll have a positive impact on other aspects of your life.

I'm a gym rat. There's a time for those types of workouts and I love them, but that's not what I'm talking about here. When you train in nature, I promise you will feel better mentally and physically. It's not about the intensity.

This doesn't take any skill, expertise, or money. It simply takes you getting up, getting dressed, and starting to move around. Create your flow. Move, stretch, breathe, walk, run, roll around. I'm talking about simple, basic, natural, primal movement that repairs, restores, replenishes and reenergizes you.

Alone, or with a friend, your spouse, or your kids . . . that's your call.

Personally, I use this time for me. I do way more than enough each week surrounded by people for work, fitness, family, and kids' school stuff and activities. None of that is bad; it's just enough.

- Put your headphones and listen to *The Midlife Male* (or another great podcast).
- Use voice memos to set your intention or to-do list for the day, week, month.
- Dictate that email or memo response that you want to get off your chest but will never send (I do this all the time).
- Just observe and take in your surroundings.

I wasn't always doing this. In fact, I was rarely doing this for many, many years. I had the same goals as I do now: to feel better, have a better outlook, reduce tension and stress, exert energy, clear my head. But my application was all wrong. I thought you had to go harder to achieve all those things. What I found is that once I started to back off and take more active recovery days, once I got outside of the gym, the studios, the noise, and the intensity, my mind and body started to feel and perform better.

You don't need a fancy gym, the best equipment, a boutique studio, the perfect lighting or playlist, the latest, greatest, trendiest, most IG-friendly selfie spot. You just need some outdoor space, a little heart, effort, consistency, and discipline. Then you can get in the best *overall* condition of your life.

Walk and talk

We are not made to be locked inside a cubicle all day. We are biologically built to move around and get in touch with the outdoors. Our bodies need to experience changes in air, temperature, and scenery to interrupt the stagnant office environment.

Fortunately, we live in a time where Wi-Fi and laptops and an increasing postpandemic acceptance of flexible work environments make it possible for those of us who do most of our work on the computer and phone (which is to say almost all of us) to change up our surroundings. There are plenty of benefits to taking your work outdoors.

When's the last time you took a walk and talked?

Not on your phone.

An actual "let's go for a walk and talk." Man to man. Face to face.

I spent much of one Friday at Evelyn's Park near my home in Houston. It was a beautiful day, and I just wanted to be outside.

That doesn't mean I was slacking off, skipping work, or wasting the day.

For me, I function better when I'm in nature. I don't sit still very well or for very long. Being able to move helps me to be more productive and get more accomplished.

I must've done twenty laps around the park. I walked and I talked. I was very fortunate to have had three different people meet me at the park to join me.

Trapping ourselves indoors has created what health experts call a "nature deficit disorder"—depression or anxiety resulting from too little time spent outside. Getting outdoors reduces stress, lowers blood pressure, and improves immune function. What's more, incorporating elements of nature into your workday can also give your brain a boost, resulting in increased productivity, focus, and creativity.

Harvard physician Dr. Eva M. Selhub, coauthor of *Your Brain on Nature*, says a drop of nature is like a drop of morphine to the brain, since it "stimulates reward neurons in your brain. It turns off the stress response, which means you have lower cortisol levels, lower heart rate and blood pressure, and improved immune response."

While Selhub says spending twenty minutes a day outdoors is recommended, studies have shown even looking at photographs of nature can deliver some of the same cognitive benefits as physically being outdoors.

I think people open up outdoors. Discomfort, anxiety, and competition that mark many office or boardroom settings give way to a more pleasing, mutually beneficial relationship environment.

Whether alone or with others, working or working out, the common denominator is clear: the great outdoors can be a big help when you're creating a much-needed environmental shift.

Get Moving

Tips for merging work and the outdoors

Take meetings out of the office. Hosting meetings outdoors is an easy way to get your daily dose of nature without taking a break from the job. By removing yourself from familiar office surroundings, you can literally step outside the box and feel freer to brainstorm ideas. Jeff Fitzhugh, one of my favorite people and CEO of RAEN optics, talked about the value of getting out and walking when he was on *The Midlife Male* podcast. If his team really wants to talk to him, he says, they join him on his walk. Once, my colleague suggested we get coffee for a walk and talk. I built an entire day around that invitation.

Sweatworking is the new networking. I do much better in workout clothes than I do in a business suit. I realize there's a time and place for both in my business. However, inviting certain clients and prospects to meet for workouts has proved highly effective, fun, and motivating. It gets results, both healthwise and businesswise. It builds camaraderie, increases communication, and encourages overcoming adversity together.

Take your laptop outdoors. Working at the park or an outdoor café can provide the mental stimulation required to get through the day. First, you can set up an outdoor workspace anywhere these days. Pretty much everywhere has Wi-Fi, and you can even use your phone as a hotspot. An antiglare screen is huge, as it will allow you to minimize the brightness of the sun and still enjoy the benefits of fresh air, greenery, and ambient light.

Grab a meal and go. Since we know eating at your desk is bad for your health, lunchtime is a great opportunity to grab a breath of fresh air along with your meal. It's also a natural incentive to eat healthier. You're outside, the weather is nice, you're feeling good. You tend to order and eat a bit better.

What to Do on Vacation

You do take vacations, right? If you're not maxing out your vacation days, that's the first thing you need to change! And that doesn't mean you need to travel; the "staycation" can be just as valuable.

Easiest list I've ever made . . .

- Train
- Spend lots of time outdoors
- Take walks
- Hold hands
- Watch the sunrise and sunset
- Swim
- Eat really good food
- Try something new
- Buy something
- Read
- Write
- Check in with office once a day
- Talk with your kids
- Put your phone down
- Sleep well

CHAPTER 29

Getting a Late Start Is Better Than Not Starting at All

Stay curious to keep growing.

Retirement is just a concept. As I meet more interesting people, I've been able to maintain a curiosity that has taken me into all of these different realms, out of my normal comfort zones of what I thought I was an expert on and being in different circles with different people. People always evolve. I'm always going to be working on this project or that project. I can't imagine just sitting around thinking, OK, I'm in my sixties, and I'm just chillin', and these are the golden years. Fuck that. I want those years to be as high performing as all the others. When I was in my twenties, I was married at the time and thought I was super happy, and I remember thinking, oh, my thirties are going to be so easy. Everything got turned on its head. I went through a shitty divorce.

I moved across the country from LA to New York. There is no cruise control, and you need those things—as shitty as they seem. Those moments in your life are a reminder of what you're made of, what you can do, and how much potential you have left.

People sell themselves short. The old mindset of our parents was that you showed up, you did this job, and you did that thing every day for twenty years, and you get a gold watch and a pension at the end of it. First of all, that world doesn't exist anymore, but also thank God that you can start a podcast. You can talk to people about things that are interesting. The reach is so great now with social media and all the different platforms. I've developed insane amounts of business connections through Instagram. That didn't even exist ten years ago. I can make a video and have it out in the world in two seconds and not have to ask permission or wait for someone to tell me, "We pick you." I came from the world of performing and acting and dancing. You'd get in a room, and you'd wait for somebody to get in the room and give you permission. Now I'm like, "Fuck that. No, I'm taking ownership of this. I'm taking the power back." That's the amazing thing. There's so many avenues and so much to do. You're the only limiting factor.

— **DEAN SHEREMET,** chef, wellness expert, dancer, TV personality, and author of *Eat Your Heart Out: The Look Good, Feel Good, Silver Lining Cookbook,* on *The Midlife Male* podcast, Episode #145

* * *

The experiences we have in our life almost never go the way we scripted them. Agreed? When you hit forty, you've gained a shitload of experience. That should be your launching pad. And if you missed it, don't cry about it. Just start *now*. It's the single easiest and best advice I've ever gotten.

Makes sense. There is no perfect time . . . never is, never will be.

We live in a different world than our dads did, where—although nothing is guaranteed—we can reasonably expect to be learning and applying lessons over a longer stretch of time. In midlife, you have a lot better understanding of who you are, where you want to go, and what is realistic, yet you're still young enough to take action and enjoy the ride. If we're going to be living longer . . . healthier . . . better . . . that's a lot of runway ahead. If you think the best is behind you once you hit your forties and fifties, that's not a winning strategy. Flip the script. The middle is the sweet spot. We're just getting started.

Embrace curiosity

I love the word curiosity. Embrace it or die.

Curiosity gives you the motivation to stay in motion, going new places and trying new things.

You know what keeps guys from being curious and trying new things? We're afraid of looking ridiculous, especially in a bullshit social media world where we're supposed to look perfect. News flash for you: I didn't have my shit together in my twenties or thirties, and now I'm supposed to take advice from some twenty-year-old influencer with a life hack?! Hell, no!

It's OK to suck. Trust me. Part of the fun is embracing the suck. Laugh at yourself, or turn the suck into mastery by really getting into it. Put your testosterone in the drawer, get out there, and take the chance you just might embarrass yourself.

Perfection is an illusion

I've been *that* guy—the guinea pig, trial-and-error, success-and-failure-over-and-over-again, give-it-a-shot guy.

I've been that guy who had to have all the answers, own every conversation, win every negotiation, and who believed that I had control over things, could handle it all, and could chase down what I wanted or outrun what I didn't.

I'm also the guy who can attest that pretty much nothing I believed and pretty much none of the actions that I was taking were resulting in better relationships, better health, better finances, better business, or better almost anything. Yet, while all of this was going on internally in my life, from the outside looking in, you would have had no idea. On paper and in pictures, it all looked pretty good. I don't think I'm alone here:

- You're in good shape.
- You have a beautiful family.
- Your kids are going to private school.
- You live in a nice house.
- You're driving nice cars.
- You dress well.
- You look pretty popular, surrounded by friends.

All of this can be true, and for all intents and purposes, it is, but you can also be completely unfulfilled:

- You could also feel like you're in complete disarray and out of balance.
- You could be winning daily battles yet losing the war on life.
- You could be overcomplicating pretty much everything.
- You could be in denial and ignoring all of the signs that tell you over and over again that what you're doing is not sustainable and isn't working.
- You are chasing instead of letting things happen.
- You are focusing on the wrong things.
- You are doing things for others before yourself.
- You are doing things that are inauthentic to you by nature.
- You're pushing the sale.
- You're talking when you should be listening.
- You are overtraining.
- You are under-resting.
- You're following instead of leading, and you sure as shit are not really practicing what you preach.

Like many of you, I was just doing a lot of different shit—throwing it against the wall and trying to see what would stick.

I was rudderless. When you've got no direction, you'll take your cues from what others ask of you, whether they have your best interests at heart or not. You'll avoid conflict, kick the can down the road on problems, and ignore what you know you should do:

- Oh, you want me to be this type of person, and maybe you'll buy from me? Great. *I'll try to chameleon myself into that kind of person for a little while.*

- Oh, I need to be at this event tonight, and I need to be up early the next morning? *Yeah, I can do both.*

- Oh, we went out to dinner as a family. We said seven words to each other, took a great photo. Boom. Check the box. *That's not quality time and communication.*

- Oh, I wrote a bunch of new business this year, stayed in The Presidents Club, and accomplished my "goal."

But what wasn't I doing? What choices was I making?

- Did I reach out and help anybody else achieve their goal?

- Did I not find the time to talk to that financial advisor?

- Did I not reach out to that friend I hadn't talked to in a while?

- Did I still find the time to make one more stop at Lululemon on the way home to buy something I absolutely didn't need so that I could get that temporary dopamine retail-therapy rush that made me feel good because goddammit, this week I earned it?

You're responsible for your results

When you really get down to it and pull your head out of your ass, it's all on you to continue to work on yourself. I can tell you the following with 100 percent certainty: *you are the only one who can truly help you achieve the happiness and the life that you want.*

You can surround yourself with great people in every one of these areas: coaching, therapy, food, fitness. You can join the boards of various charities.

These are all positive things, but unless you are truly committed to getting uncomfortable and doing the hard work on yourself, it doesn't matter.

I've got advice to share, and every week I learn more from my successful and flawed Midlife Male guests who have done amazing things in all sorts of endeavors, personally and professionally. And guess what? They're also just trying to figure it out like the rest of us. They bring different viewpoints, philosophies, and things that you can employ in your day-to-day life. I encourage you to try them and listen to these guys. But don't get me wrong here. These tips do not take the place of doing the actual work.

Streamlining your wardrobe will make you feel a little bit better, give you a little bit more confidence.

Making some more money will provide you some opportunities that you didn't have before that you could enjoy.

Saving some more money will give you a level of confidence and freedom that you didn't have before.

Eating better will give you more energy and health benefits.

Spending some time on your fitness will improve just about everything.

Using a great face wash will make your skin more radiant.

Insert your own thing that you know you should be doing here and you're just not.

At the core, however, at the true depth of all of it, you need to believe in yourself.

You need to work on yourself daily, and the work needs to be authentic and wired straight to who you are, what you are about, and who you want to be.

If it's not genuine, vulnerable, and transparent, if you can't wear it on your sleeve every day as a true representation of your identity, then none of the other superficial, overcomplicated possessions, trappings of success, or false positives are going to provide satisfaction. I do not care what age or what stage of life you're in right now.

You might be getting a late start, but it's not too late.

I was told this at dinner one night when I shared about something I was looking into: "Yeah, but you'd be getting a late start."

Fuck that. Do not ever use a late start as an excuse not to start.

Get after it.

Get Naked

Wanted: A MLM
What would you write if you were to describe yourself in a want ad? I don't mean cutting and pasting your dating app profile (or the one you used fifteen years ago). This ain't the Piña Colada song. I'm talking about how you see yourself as a Midlife Male right *now*. Are you:

- a badass with a touch of humility?
- a responsible, dependable father and husband full of unconditional love?
- an adventurous soul on a journey to enlightenment?
- a grinder, day by day, and loving it?
- creative and curious, tinkering with new ideas and skills?
- maybe a bit of all of these?

You got this.

Scheinman's Yearly Goal Setting

I do an annual goal-setting exercise for myself. Here are a few notes and tips if you decide to do the same.

- Middle-aged men still need to have goals. That's nonnegotiable if you want to keep growing and learning, yet too often our own personal goal setting gets put on the back burner behind family, career, and many other obligations and choices.
- I hit all the Fs. Not all get the same weight in a given year, but that's my choice. It's important to be aware of all areas of your life.
- Write down your goals. I use Evernote so I don't lose them and I can easily refer to it throughout the year. Maybe you're an old-school paper-and-pen guy or just want to use your phone's notepad. Just write it down.

re it with an "accountability partner"—or, you
ow . . . your actual partner or a trusted friend;
a don't have to give them a fancy title. It's just
portant to not keep this in your head; it's too
easy to run away from your goals when they are
stuck up there.

- I do this goal-setting exercise for me and me only.
  But I have bigger ideas in mind when I formulate
  some of those goals. Maybe I want to practice
  mental health so I'll be a better husband and father.
  Maybe I invest in causes and people I believe in
  because it helps them influence the world. I take
  seriously what my legacy will be generations from
  now, and goal setting helps make that happen.

Having intention is the real value in creating this list
each year. We don't do this for accolades or extra credit. It's
personal. It's planned. It's purposeful and helps us avoid
just floating through life reacting to everything swirling
around. Every action creates a reaction.

Don't wait until January 1. Do it. Your new year starts
now—there it is again . . . just start now.

Here are my daily nonnegotiables:

1. Meditate, practice gratitude, breathe.

2. Do the hard things first.

3. Revisit my endgame/goals daily.

4. Don't fuck with things that don't move the needle.

5. Be intentional.

6. Exercise.

7. Ask questions: How can I serve you? Who do you know that can help me?

8. Write for thirty to sixty minutes.

9. Read for thirty to sixty minutes.

10. Record one podcast per week.

11. Reach out to three to five clients, networks, and new people, and connect the dots each week.

Here's how I goal set and write shit down:

☐ Invest in three to five companies/brands I'm passionate about, led by people I love.

☐ Focus on *quality* clients/relationships over quantity.

☐ Prepay all taxes.

☐ Stay on a monthly budget.

☐ Plan trips for weekends and the year.

☐ Take part in three new events/challenges.

☐ Develop a uniform. Streamline wardrobe to reduce shopping/anxiety.

☐ Home—invest in a few new pieces to enhance quality of life.

☐ Have quarterly "goals" meeting with boys and Kate to help figure out our priorities and what's important—

camp, sports, education, travel, money—so that we can be better as a family.

- [ ] Train functional, flexible, longevity-based fitness surrounded by like-minded people to live, perform, and think better.

- [ ] Limit/minimize distractions and negativity.

- [ ] Read and listen more.

- [ ] Meditate daily.

- [ ] Have sex two to three times per week.

- [ ] Say *no* to anything that does not contribute to achieving the above goals!

EPILOGUE

The Seventh F: "Filanthropy"

I've come to this aha moment ever since the Southwest Airlines incident that if I had not made it through that day and my life would have just ended right there, I would have been so upset with myself for allowing myself to be reactive to everything else except for my own ambitions and hopes and aspirations.

I was on a Southwest flight that was traveling out of New York City to Dallas. I do a lot of work in New York City. I probably fly there forty-five times a year. We do a lot of work at the United Nations around sustainable energy. This was a routine flight. I take it so often. I remember booking that flight from Dallas to New York City on late Sunday night. It was basically Monday morning, and I booked it at like 1:30 in the morning to get that 6:00 a.m. flight to New York City. I was there for less than twenty-four hours. I had a couple meetings at the UN and then hopped back on a flight. I was up in the air for nineteen or so minutes. I recall laying my head against the window.

Normally I try to take advantage of every ounce of productivity that I have, so if I can be online, I'm going to be online and get done whatever I need to get done. Normally when they make the sound, "ding," and you can open up your laptops, I'm the first one. But this time I remember being exhausted and thought I'd wait a little bit. I was on the window seat on the right side of the plane and remember laying my head against it.

What startled me and everyone on that plane was a loud boom. It was a boom so loud that everybody kind of looked around at each other, like, "Did you hear that?" But we all gave that look and it all happened so fast that before anyone could even utter a word, we hear another loud explosion. That explosion was two and a half rows away from me. There was a hole on the side of the plane. As you can imagine, chaos ensued. I vividly remember the oxygen masks being deployed from the top. I'd never had to see them before, but I saw them deploy across the cabin. People are screaming, the wind is roaring. It was an incredibly frightening experience.

I'm a firm believer that in life we go through different seasons. Not every season requires the grind, but there are some seasons where you've got to grind—it's just not sustainable to do that over the period of a career. I've realized many things from that flight incident, but it's really forced me to reevaluate how I do things and if I'm doing the right things. One of the big things is focusing on myself first. I've only developed that habit over the past year consistently.

I made all the mistakes that the founder of any company has made, if not more. The first thing I used to do when I'd *wake up in the morning was pick up my phone and I'd look at my emails. And immediately, I'm now a pinball. Whatever I had planned for the day, immediately that fire sitting in my email inbox is now my priority. I'd immediately jump up, get dressed and go to work, and then I'd grind. I learned over the years that it's not sustainable.*

Now when I wake up in the morning, I have to do something for myself first. I'm not going to look at emails and things like that, because I'm a better leader and teacher, a better CEO, a better brother and son, a better friend, better everything, if I make time for myself first. I get those endorphins going and I feel so on my game.

Now I've been considering the idea of taking a trip by myself to someplace I've never been with a blank journal. I'm in the season of life of self-discovery. I really, really, really want to understand myself in a better way, and I think I'll do that by taking myself out of the work for a little bit and allowing the silence to unravel my mental side.

— **MARTY MARTINEZ,** founder and CEO of Social Revolt Agency, on *The Midlife Male* podcast, Episode #87

* * *

Marty and his fellow passengers went through a harrowing ordeal on April 17, 2018, Flight 1380 from LaGuardia to Dallas. One woman died after being hit by debris from a failed engine that shot into the cabin—the first airline fatality in the United States since 2009. Seven others were injured. Pilot Tammie Jo Shults was hailed as a hero for taking the Boeing 737 into rapid descent for an emergency landing in Philadelphia.

Marty was only twenty-nine years old when he used Wi-Fi to get on Facebook Live to record what he thought would be his final moments as the plane was going down.

"I was cataloging the last few minutes that I thought I would be alive," Marty told the *Dallas Morning News*. "It was terrifying."

He is still a long way from Midlife Male age, but *that* will give you some damn perspective.

I hope you understand what he's saying here when he talks about doing something for himself. He's not talking about being selfish. He's talking about self-care. He's talking about what my friends and I have been talking about in all 29 chapters of this book.

You know how flight attendants and self-help authors tell you that you have to put on your own oxygen mask before you can help others? Marty, who had his oxygen mask on as smoke poured into that plane, is quite literally telling you to put on your oxygen mask first.

This whole book has been about unraveling the mental side—and physical, financial, emotional, spiritual, and relationship sides—of your life. Unravel. Peel back the layers of the onion. Get naked. If you want to make a positive difference in your life and the lives of those around you, take care of yourself, and get real about the man you want to be.

Nothing in this book is my foolproof, 100 percent guaranteed recipe for success. I've given you some suggestions. I've told you what I've found works and doesn't work for me—after many years of trial and error. The hard work in maximizing middle age is up to you.

And it starts now.

What is success to you?

What relationships do you want to cultivate, and which ones should you dial back?

What's really important to you in your family, your career, your projects, and your passions?

How much time do you need for yourself as opposed to generating energy and inspiration for others?

What do you want your legacy to be?

We've spent this book discussing how to embrace the six Fs in our lives. There's a seventh F that is fitting to end with—filanthropy, or philanthropy if you like to spell correctly. I'm way in the deep end with the Fs, so I'm not changing it now. You get to do that when you write your own book.

In some ways, filanthropy is the whole ball game. Why improve yourself with family and friends, fitness, fashion, food, fun, and finance if you don't use that knowledge, common sense, and charisma to make the world a better place? Your legacy will play out long after you're gone, but taking filanthropy seriously while you're alive is how you prepare the soil for that legacy to grow.

Filanthropy can be defined broadly, and you should consider what drives you and how you are uniquely situated to make a difference to others. Your goals may be large or modest, but take your task seriously, and also have fun with it. You may be surprised at what you challenge yourself to accomplish. It doesn't have to mean huge gifts and donations. How do you want to give back and contribute to the world?

I can tell you from my perspective that I know I'm not putting a man on the moon, curing cancer, or creating a zero-emissions energy source. I want to lead by example for my boys and set them on their best paths to help them see the dangers they encounter and do honorable battle with them. I want them to respect themselves and others, to see value in all these Fs, even though finding balance across all of them can seem elusive. I want to spread a message of hope, grace, and strength—strength defined the way I see it, which unites people so we can collaborate and help each other live to our fullest. That's the bandwidth I have *here*. It's what I can control *here*.

What I find cool to think about is that you'll never know how great your impact will be, or even when that impact will be felt. You do the best you can and let the rest take care of itself. And you do it without expecting to receive a report card with your final results. That's not part of the deal.

At the start of this book, I asked you to stand in front of the mirror. I said to you, "The next time you get out of the shower, find a mirror—full length, if you can. Am I asking you to be naked and afraid? Not at all. I'm inviting you to be naked and aware."

I've seen some version of this quote attributed to a lot of people: "Courage isn't the absence of fear. It's being afraid and doing it anyway." Awareness is similar: it's the ability to see your worst flaws and push ahead to improve them anyway.

So what do you see now?

Do you see strength where before you saw scars?

Do you see opportunity where you used to see fear?

Do you see hope for a brighter future? Remember . . . midlife is the sweet spot in the middle. You still have a lifetime ahead of you—whether you die tomorrow or in fifty-five years. What are you going to do with it?

Get Moving

I started going on a lot of business trips, and I have, I would say, a mild fear of flying. It's not overwhelmingly bad, but it's enough that it makes people around me say, "What's the matter with you? Get yourself together." Every time on these trips, I was fascinated by this idea—my girls at that time were four and three years old—it didn't matter how much time I'd spent with them, how much love I gave them, how much we laughed and shared those moments, if the plane went down during that trip, then the girls wouldn't remember a single thing about me. That really hit me to my core. It didn't make these flights very pleasant, I must say, but this idea that they wouldn't have anything to remember me, and more important what I would want to tell and advise them about life's challenges in the years ahead, that was the impetus for writing the book. From those moments on, I decided I would devote every free time I had to the book.

— **MARK HSU,** author of *Please Open in the Event of My Death: A Father's Advice to His Daughters in Case Something Horrible Happens (Which Hopefully It Won't But Just in Case . . .)*, on *The Midlife Male* podcast, Episode #122

* * *

Did you ever do one of those activities in class or summer camp or Sunday school where you write a letter to your future self . . . like when you would be fifty years old? Don't look now: if your AARP card isn't already in your wallet, it's in the mail.

What might you have written to yourself then? Did it resemble what you've become, and would that young boy be proud of what he's looking at now?

Mark took a similar concept and turned it into a book for his daughters. Mark says that people have told him after reading his book that they have written letters for their own children to open at a later date. Or they write emails that are scheduled to be delivered to themselves years later.

My dad taught me a lot, but there was plenty more he never got a chance to. I wish he had taught me to play poker before my frat brothers took all my money first semester. And I wish it hadn't taken me so damn long to learn how to tie an acceptable tie. Even a half Windsor is a bitch.

My mom, because she's half pack rat and all angel, saved all kinds of writing that my dad did when I was a kid, especially after he got diagnosed with cancer. She made sure notes he wrote to my brothers and me, letters he wrote me at summer camp and in the short time I was at college before he passed—as well as letters I wrote back to him—were preserved.

What a gift that is.

Communicate with your loved ones in any way you can, and don't forget that you have a chance to make sure you contribute to their lives long after you're gone.

Make those words count.

ACKNOWLEDGMENTS

don't even know how I managed to write a book, much less pour my heart out trying to write proper acknowledgments to the very special friends, family, colleagues, and others who have helped make all of this possible. There's no way I'll do y'all justice and put into words exactly how I feel, but please know that I am humbled, grateful, and very fortunate to have you and the experiences we've shared as part of my journey.

I've forgotten some people and left out many for a variety of reasons. If you're reading this and thinking it's you, it likely is. That's all part of me still working on my many issues. I appreciate your patience with me and acceptance of my thanks. Everyone I've ever encountered and had an experience with—good, bad or indifferent—has helped me get here.

Thank you to Kate Marie Scheinman. There's not one part of this book that does not have something to do with you in one way, shape, or form. There's also not one part of this book that you've actually read—but to use your words right back to you: "I don't need to read it, Greg, I'm living it!" You are the most secure, comfortable-in-your-own-skin, beautiful, and compelling person I know. I am blessed to share this life with you and our boys.

Thank you to my boys: Auden and Harper. You are my world. There is no better job in the world than being your father. I cherish every moment that we've shared together, hold on deeply to every memory I have with each of you, and look forward to every experience that lies ahead for us. You are the greatest gifts in my life. As my father wrote to me in his last letter, "There are many men with more money than I, but none can feel any richer than I do when I look at you and your brother." I know I embarrass you by sharing your stories, being called "the midlife male" by your friends, and putting so much out there. But I do it with so much pride and with hope that it helps other dads out there to understand the unconditional love that I have from being a father.

Thank you to my dad: Alan Gary Scheinman. There was simply no one better. A boy and his dad. I needed you. I still need you. I love you.

Thank you to my brothers: Sandy and Jarret. We are different. We are unique. We are family, and I love you both.

Thank you to my mother, Roni: You've shown generosity, care, concern, and love to your fullest capacity and have always done the best you can. For that, I love you.

Thank you to my Aunt Lenore: You have become one of my closest friends. You're my dad's sister, and his memory lives on through you. I do my best to care for you the way he would have. You are kind, sweet, and a wonderful sounding board and voice of reason. I love you very much.

Thank you, Phil: You are the most selfless person I know. You simply always do the right thing and never ask for anything in return. You have helped us get a home, been "Poppy" to our boys, and been a mentor, friend, and father figure to me. You've also been a wonderful husband to my mother. I love you and thank you from the bottom of my heart.

Thank you, Naren Aryal . . . Man, what can I say? If you would've told me that we'd be friends, confidantes, advisors, therapists—with daily phone calls to bitch, moan, complain and brag about our kids—twenty-plus years after being side-by-side competitors in the children's entertainment business, I'd have told you to bet the under because that ain't gonna fuckin' happen. But here we are, doing a book together. Seriously, I love you man. You are a stellar human being, father, publisher, entrepreneur, class act, and friend. I couldn't have done this without you. Thank you to you and your team at Amplify. Y'all are truly the best.

Thank you, Myles Schrag: I miss our weekly calls where we were supposed to be talking about the book and we went off on hour-long tangents where I just threw up all over you and you somehow turned it into all sorts of amazing content. You complete me, brotha—like, literally complete my sentences. Or at least turn them into something that makes me sound somewhat coherent and compelling. You're a total pro, incredible writing partner, and a pleasure to work with. I consider you a true friend.

Thank you to the many people who shared ideas, read early drafts of the manuscript, and provided testimonials, feedback, coaching, support, and friendship. I'm lookin' at JT, Doug Cohen, Kirk Moquin, Josh Linkner, Rich Kleiman,

Seamus Mullen, Jeff Agostinelli, Dose and Taj Khan, Will Morris, Lionel McBee, Paul Epstein, Brian Gallagher, Joel "Thor" Neeb, John Redell, and Jody Johnston.

Thank you to all the Midlife Males out there. What started as a side hustle has evolved into a movement. We're inspiring men—and in the process, we have built a growing business with the power to change lives. You've given me a voice and a platform to do what I love and to not only be able to share it with you through this book, the podcast, and the newsletter, but to do it in service of you.